BELLY LAUGHS FOR ALL!

Adult Version
Volume 6

ROBERTA CAVA

Copyright © 2016 by Roberta Cava

All rights reserved. No part of this work covered by the copyrights hereon may be reproduced or used in any form or by any means - graphic, electronic or mechanical, including photocopying, recording, taping or information storage and retrieval systems - without the prior written permission of the publisher.

Belly Laughs for All!

Adult Version

Volume 6

Roberta Cava

Published by Cava Consulting

info@dealingwithdifficultpeople.info

Discover other titles by Roberta Cava at
www.dealingwithdifficultpeople.info

National Library of Australia

Cataloguing-in-publication data:

ISBN 978-0-9944365-4-2

BOOKS BY ROBERTA CAVA

Non-Fiction

Dealing with Difficult People
(23 publishers - in 17 languages)
Dealing with Difficult Situations – at Work and at Home
Dealing with Difficult Spouses and Children
Dealing with Difficult Relatives and In-Laws
Dealing with Domestic Violence and Child Abuse
Dealing with School Bullying
Dealing with Workplace Bullying
Retirement Village Bullies
New: Keeping our children safe
What am I going to do with the rest of my life?
Before tying the knot – Questions couples Must ask each other Before they marry!
How Women can advance in business
Survival Skills for Supervisors and Managers
Human Resources at its Best!
Human Resources Policies and Procedures
Employee Handbooks
Easy Come – Hard to go – The Art of Hiring, Disciplining and Firing Employees
Time and Stress – Today's silent killers
Take Command of your Future – Make things Happen
Belly Laughs for All! – Volumes 1 to 6
Wisdom of the World

Fiction

That Something Special
Something Missing
Trilogy: Life Gets Complicated
Life Goes On
Life Gets Better

BELLY LAUGHS FOR ALL!

Volume 6

Table of Contents

INTRODUCTION	1
CHAPTER 1 – MALES	3
CHAPTER 2 – FEMALES	11
CHAPTER 3 – COUPLES	17
CHAPTER 4 – POLITICS	29
CHAPTER 5 – DOCTORS	51
CHAPTER 6 – POLICE	57
CHAPTER 7 – TRAVEL	65
CHAPTER 8 – CHILDREN	73
CHAPTER 9 – SENIORS	85
CHAPTER 10 – BLONDES	105
CHAPTER 11 – RELIGION	109
CHAPTER 12 – AT WORK	121

CHAPTER 13 – IS THAT RIGHT?	**133**
CHAPTER 14 – MISCELLANEOUS	**149**
CHAPTER 15 – HISTORY	**163**
CHAPTER 16 – BAR	**175**
CHAPTER 17 – HIGH TECHNOLOGY	**181**
CHAPTER 18 – RULES FOR LIVING	**191**
CHAPTER 19 – ON THE SERIOUS SIDE	**195**
CONCLUSION -	**203**

INTRODUCTION

Most of my books relate to how to deal with difficult people and situations. I had been feeling very depressed after writing my last three books - which focused around bullying - at home, at school and at work. This was a lovely change from that disturbing and depressing research.

I had collected jokes for years and enjoyed reading them whenever I felt down-in-the-dumps. This is what stimulated me to write books on humour. It was soon evident that I had too many jokes for just one volume, hence I wrote Volumes 1, 2, 3, 4, 5 and this is Volume 6. They discuss humour in different areas, so there's no repetition. I also realised that the books were meant for adult audiences and ***are not suitable for children***.

I hope you enjoy this volume enough to want to obtain the other five volumes.

CHAPTER 1

MALE JOKES

New baby:

A week after giving birth, a new mom went out for a break and left the baby at home with her husband. It was only a short while before the baby started to cry. The perplexed father tried all of the tricks that he remembered his wife doing, but to no avail. Finally, after half an hour in desperation he went to the doctor. After checking off all the regular things, the doctor discovered it was just a dirty diaper.

'I don't understand,' the father exclaimed, 'I knew it was dirty, but the diaper package said specifically that it was good up to three kilograms.'

Problem at home:

A man came home from work and found his five children playing in the mud in the yard. He also noted that they were still in their pajamas. He also saw empty takeaway food boxes strewn around the garden.

As he walked in the door, he found an even bigger mess. The family room was strewn with toys, and dishes filled the sink in the kitchen.

He headed upstairs, stepping over piles of dirty clothes. When he rushed to the bedroom he found his wife still curled up in bed still in her pajamas reading a novel.

She looked up at him, smiled and asked how his day went. He looked at her in bewilderment and asked, 'What happened here today?'

She again smiled and answered, 'You know every day when you come home from work and you ask me what in the world I do all day?'

'Yes,' was his incredulous reply.

She answered, 'Well, today I didn't do it.'

Vegetables:

His wife asked him to buy organic vegetables at the market. He looked around and couldn't find any, so grabbed an older, tired-looking employee and asked, 'These vegetables are for my wife. Have they been sprayed with any poisonous chemicals?'

The produce guy looked at him and replied, 'No. You'll have to do that yourself.'

Geraniums:

The owner of the flower shop said, 'I'm sorry sir, we don't have potted geraniums. Could you use lilies instead?

The customer replied sadly, 'No, it was geraniums my wife told me to water while she was away.'

Say you're sorry:

Son, 'Dad, I want to get married.'
Father, 'First, tell me you're sorry.'
Son, 'For what?'
Father, 'Say sorry.'
Son, 'But for what? What did I do?'
Father, 'Just say sorry.
Son, 'But... what have I done wrong?'
Father, 'Say sorry!'
Son, 'Please, just tell me why?'
Father, 'Say sorry...'
Son, Okay dad, I'm sorry.'
Father, 'There! You've finished training. When you learn to say sorry for no reason at all, then you're ready to get married.'

Missing wife:

My wife has been missing a week now. The police said to prepare for the worst. So, I had to go down to Lifeline and get all of her clothes back.

So hot:

'It's just too hot to wear clothes today,' Jack said as he stepped out of the shower. 'Honey, what do you think the neighbours would think if I mowed the lawn lie this?'

'Probably that I married you for your money,' she replied.

Guided tour:

I met a Chinese girl when I was in Shanghai and asked her if she would escort me for a city tour. I asked her for her mobile number so I could call her.

She got excited and said, 'Sex sex sex want free sex for to night.'

Wow! I'm guessing this is how Chinese women express hospitality! But then my friend interpreted for me and told me that what she really said was, 666 1236 429.

The blind man:

A blind man walks into a store with his seeing eye dog. All of a sudden, he picks up the leash and begins swinging the dog over his head.

The manager runs up to the man and asks, 'What are you doing?!'

The blind man replies, 'Just looking around.'

Nicknames:

I was listening to the radio this morning when the host invited callers to reveal the nicknames they had for their wives. The best call was from a brave fella who called his wife, 'Harvey Norman.'

The host asked him why that name. He replied, 'Absolutely no interest for 36 months.'

The new girlfriend:

Paddy thought his new girlfriend might be the one, but after looking through her knickers drawer and finding a nurse's outfit, a French maid's outfit, and a police woman's uniform, he finally decided if she couldn't hold down a job, she wasn't the one for him.

GPS

Jim says, 'When you visit us tomorrow – do you need directions?'

Andy, 'I'm all set. I have the address, a GPS and a GPS override.'

Jim replies, 'What's a GPS override?'

Andy, 'My wife.'

New pup:

I received this ad from a friend of mine. He really could use your help.

The ad reads: This is Lexi. She's an 8-week-old German Sheppard, I bought Lexi as a surprise for my wife, but it turns out she's allergic to dogs so we are now looking to find her a new home.

She's 39-years-old, a beautiful and caring woman who drives, is a great cook and keeps a good house.

Men's help line:

'Hello, you've reached the Men's Help Line. My name is Bob. How can I help you?'

'Hi Bob, I really need your advice on a serious problem. I have suspected for some time now that my wife has been cheating on me. You know, just the usual signs… The phone rings and when I answer, the caller hangs up. Plus, she goes out with 'the girls' quite a lot. I usually try to stay awake to look out for her when she comes home, but I always fall asleep.

Anyway, last night about midnight, I woke up and she wasn't home. So I hid in the garage behind my boat and waited for her. When she came home, she got out of someone's car, buttoning her blouse, then she took her panties out of her purse and slipped them on.

It was at that moment, while crouched behind the boat, that I noticed a hairline crack in the outboard motor mounting bracket. Is that something I can weld or do I need to replace the whole bracket?'

They say your partner usually resembles your parents:

Thomas is 32 years old and he is still single. One day a friend asked, 'Why aren't you married? Can't you find a woman who will be a good wife?'

Thomas replied, 'Actually, I've found many women I wanted to marry, but when I bring them home to meet my parents, my mother doesn't like them.'

His friend thinks for a moment and says, 'I've got the perfect solution, just find a girl who's just like your mother.'

A few months later they meet again and his friend says, 'Did you find the perfect girl? Did your mother like her?'

With a frown on his face, Thomas answers, 'Yes, I found the perfect girl. She was just like my mother. You were right, my mother liked her very much.'

The friend said, 'Then what's the problem?'

Thomas replied, 'My father didn't like her.'

Dead wives:

A bus full of housewives going on a picnic, fell into a river, and all died. Each husband cried for a week. One husband continued for more than two weeks! When asked did he miss his wife so much, he replied miserably: 'No! My wife missed the bus!'

Calories burned during sex:

[I thought you might find the following data of interest.]

Removing her clothes:
    With her consent — 12 calories
    Without her consent — 2,187 calories

Opening her bra:
    With both hands — 8 calories
    With one hand — 12 calories
    With your teeth — 485 calories

Putting on a condom:
    With an erection — 6 calories
    Without an erection — 3,315 calories

Positions:
    Missionary — 12 calories
    69 lying down — 78 calories
    69 standing up — 812 calories
    Wheelbarrow — 216 calories
    Chandelier — 2,912 calories

Orgasms:
    Real — 112 calories
    Fake — 1.315 calories

Post Orgasms:
    Lying in bed hugging — 18 calories
    Getting up immediately — 36 calories
    Explaining why you got out of bed immediately — 816 calories

Getting a second erection (if you are):
    20-19 years — 36 calories
    30-39 years — 80 calories
    40-49 years — 124 calories'

50-59 years	1,972 calories
60-69 years	7,916 calories
70+	Results pending

Dressing afterwards:

Calmly	32 calories
In a hurry	98 calories
Father knocking at door	5,218 calories
Husband knocking at door	13,521 calories

P.S.: Results can vary.

Smart dog

A man went to visit a friend and was amazed to find him playing chess with his dog. He watched the game in astonishment for a while.

'I can hardly believe my eyes!' he exclaimed. 'That's the smartest dog I've ever seen.'

'Nah, he's not so smart,' the friend replied. 'I've beaten him three games out of five.'

The break-in:

I woke up to go to the toilet in the middle of the night (as I often do) and I noticed a strange individual who looked suspicious with a knife in his hand, sneaking through my next door neighbour's back garden. Suddenly my neighbour came from nowhere and smacked him over the head with a shovel, killing him instantly. He then dug a grave in the vegie patch and put the body in it and covered it.

Astonished, I got back into bed. As I tossed and turned my wife said, 'You're upset, what is it?'

'You'll never believe what I've just seen,' I said.

'What?' she said.

'That bugger next door has still got my shovel.'

Pantyhose:

A golfer was in the golf club change room and he noticed his mate changing and saw he was wearing panty hose.

He asked, 'How long have you been wearing panty hose to play golf?'

He replied. 'Ever since my wife found them in the glove box!'

Help at home:

One day my housework-challenged husband decided to wash his sweatshirt. Seconds after he stepped into the laundry room, he shouted to his wife, 'What setting do I use on the washing machine?'

'It depends,' she replied. 'What does it say on your shirt?'

'University of Sydney,' he yelled back.

Who sent you?

Even though there was a blizzard raging outside, I made it the half-mile to the bakery, where I asked the owner for six rolls.

'Your wife must love these rolls,' he said.

'How do you know these are for my wife?' I asked.

'Because I don't think your mother would send you out in weather like this.'

Being a man:

Being a male is a matter of birth;

Being a man is a matter of age;

Being a gentleman is a matter of choice.

CHAPTER 2

FEMALES

Banking problems:

A young woman ran in tears to her father and exclaimed, 'Dad, you gave me some terrible financial advice!'

'I did? What did I tell you?' asked the dad.

'You told me to put my money in that big bank and now that big bank is in trouble.'

'What are you talking about? That's one of the largest banks in the world!' he said. 'Surely there must be some mistake.'

'I don't think so,' she sniffed. 'They just returned one of my cheques with a note saying 'insufficient funds.''

All crumpled up:

With a very seductive voice, a wife asked her husband, 'Have you ever seen $20 all crumpled up?'

'No,' said her husband.

She gave him a little smile, unbuttoned the top three buttons, reached into her bra and pulled out a crumpled $20 note. She then asked, 'Have you ever seen a $50 note all crumpled up?'

'No I haven't' he said with a seductive smile.

She reached into her skirt pocket and pulled out a crumpled $50 note. 'Now,' she said, 'Have you ever seen $50,000 all crumpled up?'

'No way! He said becoming even more excited, to which she said, 'Go look in the garage.'

The best dear john letter ever:

A young girl on a year's training course in South Africa, recently received a 'Dear John' letter from her boyfriend back home. It read as follows:

Dear Mary,

I can no longer continue our relationship. The distance between us is just too great. I must admit that I have cheated on you twice, since you've been gone, and it's not fair to either of us. I'm sorry.

Please return the picture of me that I sent to you.

Love, John

Mary, with hurt feelings, asked her colleagues for any snapshots they could spare of their boyfriends, brothers, ex-boyfriends, uncles, cousins, etc. In addition to the picture of John, Mary included all the other pictures of the pretty lads she had collected from her buddies. There were 57 photos in that envelope, along with this note:

Dear John,

I'm so sorry, but I can't remember who the hell you are. Please take your picture from the pile, and send the rest back to me.

Take care, Mary

Irish furniture dealer:

Murphy, a furniture dealer from Dublin, decided to expand the line of furniture in his store, so he decided to go to Paris to see what he could find. After arriving in Paris, he visited with some manufacturers and selected a line that he thought would sell well back home. To celebrate the new acquisition, he decided to visit a small bistro and have a glass of wine.

As he sat enjoying his wine, he noticed that the small place was quite crowded, and that the other chair at his table was the only vacant seat in the house. Before long, a very beautiful young Parisian girl came to his table; asked him something in French (which Murphy couldn't understand); so he motioned to the vacant chair and invited her to sit down.

He tried to speak to her in English, but she did not speak his language. After a couple of minutes of trying to communicate with her, he took a napkin and drew a picture of a wine glass and showed it to her. She nodded, so he ordered a glass of wine for her.

After sitting together at the table for a while, he took another napkin, and drew a picture of a plate with food on it, and she nodded. They left the bistro and found a quiet cafe that featured a small group playing romantic music. They ordered dinner, after which he took another napkin and drew a picture of a couple dancing. She nodded, and they got up to dance. They danced until the cafe closed and the band was packing up.

Back at their table, the young lady took a napkin and drew a picture of a four-poster bed. To this day, Murphy has no idea how she figured out he was in the furniture business.

Why I love my Mom:

(A daughter's touching tribute she wrote to give to her Mom on Mother's Day.)

Mom and Dad were watching TV when Mom said, 'I'm tired, and it's getting late. I think I'll go to bed.'

She went to the kitchen to make sandwiches for the next day's lunches, rinsed out the popcorn bowls, took meat out of the freezer for dinner the following evening, checked the cereal box levels, filled the sugar container and put spoons and bowls on the table. She then put some wet clothes in the dryer, put a load of clothes into the washer, ironed a shirt and secured a loose button. She picked up the game pieces left on the table, put the phone back on the charger and put the telephone book into the drawer.

She watered the plants, emptied a rubbish bin and hung up a towel to dry. She yawned and stretched and headed for the bedroom. She stopped by the desk and wrote a note to the teacher, counted out some cash for a school excursion and pulled a text book out from hiding under a chair. She signed a birthday card for a friend, addressed and stamped the envelope and wrote a quick list for the grocery requirements. She put both near her purse.

Mom then washed her face, put on her night cream and age fighting moisturizer, brushed and flossed her teeth and filed her nails.

Dad called out, 'I thought you were going to bed.'

'I'm on my way,' she said as she put some water into the dog's dish and put the cat outside. She then made sure the doors were locked. She looked in on each of the kids and turned out their bedside lamps and TVs, hung up a shirt, threw some dirty socks into the basket, and had a brief conversation with the one up still doing homework.

In her own room, she set the alarm, laid out clothing for the next day, straightened up the shoe rack and added three things to her six most important things to do list. She said her prayers, and visualized the accomplishment of her goals.

About that time, Dad turned off the TV and announced to no one in particular, 'I'm going to bed.' And he did… without another thought.

Anything extraordinary here? Wonder why women live longer? Because we're made for the long haul and we can't die sooner – we still have things to do.

Women as explained by engineers:

Hazardous materials data sheet:

Element: woman
Discoverer: Adam
Atomic Mass: Accepted as 55 kg, but known to vary from 45 kg to 225 kg
Physical Properties:
1. Body surface normally covered with film of powder.
2. Boils at absolutely nothing – freezes for no apparent reason.
3. Found in various grades ranging from virgin materials to common ore.

Chemical properties:
1. Reacts well to gold, platinum and all precious stones.
2. Explodes spontaneously without reason or warning.
3. The most powerful money-reducing agent known to man.

Common use:
1. Highly ornamental, especially in sports cars.
2. Can greatly aid relaxation.
3. Can be very effective cleaning agent.

Hazards:
1. Turns green when placed alongside a superior specimen.
2. Possession of more than one is possible but specimens must never make eye contact.

William Golding said:

I think women are foolish to pretend they are equal to men. They are far superior and always have been.

Whatever you give a woman, she will make greater. If you give her sperm, she will give you a baby. If you give her a house, she'll give you a home. If you give her groceries, she'll give you a meal. If you give her a smile, she'll give you her heart. She multiplies and enlarges what is given to her. So if you give her any crap, be ready to receive a ton of shit!'

Quickie:

If your cup is only half full – you probably need a different bra.

Penny for your thoughts:

A young Scottish lad and lass were sitting on a low stone wall, holding hands, gazing out over the loch. For several minutes they sat silently. Then finally the girl looked at the boy and said, 'A penny for your thoughts, Angus.'

'Well, uh, I was thinkin'. Perhaps it's aboot time for a wee kiss.'

The girl blushed, then leaned over and kissed him lightly on the cheek. Then he blushed. The two turned once again to gaze out over the loch.

Minutes passed and the girl spoke again. 'Another penny for your thoughts, Angus?'

'Well, uh, I was thinkin' perhaps it's noo aboot time for a wee cuddle.'

The girl blushed, then leaned over and cuddled him for a few seconds. Then he blushed, and the two turned once again to gaze out over the loch. After a while, she again said, 'Another penny for your thoughts, Angus.'

'Well, uh, I was thinkin' perhaps it's aboot time you let me put my hand on your leg.'

The girl blushed, then took his hand and put it on her knee. Then he blushed. Then the two turned once again to gaze out over the loch before the girl spoke again. 'Another penny for your thoughts, Angus.'

The young man glanced down with a furrowed brow. 'Well, noo,' he said, 'my thoughts are a wee bit more serious this time.'

'Really?' said the lass in a whisper, filled with anticipation.

'Aye,' said the lad, nodding.

The girl looked away in shyness, began to blush, and bit her lip in anticipation of the ultimate request.

Then he said, 'Ye no' think it's aboot time ye paid me the first three pennies?'

CHAPTER 3

COUPLES

Debt:

A man is getting into the shower just as his wife is finishing her own shower. The doorbell rings and the wife quickly wraps herself in a towel and runs down the stairs. When she opens the door, there stands Bob, their next-door neighbour. Before she says a word, Bob says, 'I'll give you $800 if you drop that towel.'

After thinking for a moment, the woman drops her towel and stands naked in front of Bob. After a few seconds, Bob hands her $800 and leaves.

The woman re-wraps the towel around herself and goes back upstairs. When she gets to the bathroom, her husband asks, 'Who was that?'

'It was bob our next-door neighbour,' she replies sheepishly.

'Great!' her husband said, 'Did he say anything about the $800 he owes me?'

The missus:

My missus said to me the other night, 'Oh love, what did you ever do to deserve a wife like me?'

I replied, 'Goodness knows, but I won't be doing it again …'

The wife said, 'I wish I was a newspaper, so I'd be in your hands all day.'

The husband replied, 'I wish you were a newspaper too so I could get a new one every day.'

Check your e-mails:

How important it is to read your message before sending it!

A husband wrote a romantic message to his wife on his official trip and missed an 'e' in the last word. Now he is seeking police protection to enter his own house. He wrote: 'Hi darling I'm experiencing the best time of my life and I wish you were her!'

Iron troubles:

One day, Jill's husband came home from the office and found her sobbing convulsively. 'I feel terrible,' she told him. 'I was pressing your suit and I burned a big hole in the seat of your trousers.'

'Forget it,' consoled her husband. 'Remember that I bought an extra pair of pants for that suit.';

'Yes, and it's lucky for you that you did,' said Jill, drying her eyes, 'I used them to patch the hole.'

Getting weighed:

A woman noticed her husband standing on the bathroom scale, sucking in his stomach. 'Ha! That's not going to help,' she exclaimed.

'Sure it does,' he said. 'It's the only way I can see the numbers.'

Tupperware party:

One evening after dinner, a five-year-old son noticed that his mother had gone out and he asked, 'Where did mommy go?'

His father told him, 'Mommy is at a Tupperware party.'

This explanation satisfied him for only a moment. 'What's a Tupperware party, Dad?'

The man had always given my son honest answers, so he figured a simple explanation would be the best approach.

'Well, son,' he said, 'at a Tupperware party, a bunch of ladies sit around and sell plastic bowls to each other.'

He nodded, indicating that he understood this curious pastime.

Then he burst into laughter. 'Come on, Dad,' he said. 'What is it really?'

You know the romance has died when:

An elderly couple had just learned how to send text messages on their cell phones. The wife has a romantic-type of husband, a man of few words, was more of a no-nonsense guy.

One afternoon the wife went out and met a friend for coffee. She decided to send her husband a romantic text message and wrote: 'If you're sleeping, send me your dreams. If you are laughing, send me your smile. If you are eating, send me a bite. If you are drinking, send me a sip. If you are crying, send me your tears. I love you.'

The husband texted back to her: 'I'm on the toilet. Please advise.'

Change of tactics:

Every night, Harry goes out drinking. And every night, his wife, Louise, yells at him. One day, one of Louise's friends suggests that she try a different tack. 'Welcome him home with a kiss and some loving words,' she says. 'He might change his ways.'

That night, Harry stumbles back home as usual. But instead of berating him, Louise helps him into an easy chair, puts his feet up on the ottoman, removes his shoes, and gently massages his neck.

'It's late,' she whispers. 'I think we should go upstairs to bed now, don't you?'

'Might as well,' says Harry. 'I'll get in trouble if I go home.'

50th wedding anniversary:

A couple were celebrating their 50th wedding anniversary. The husband asked, 'Have you ever cheated on me? Please, I really need to know.'

'Well, all right. Yes, three times,' his wife said.

'Three? When were they?'

'Well, remember when you wanted to start a business and no bank would give you a loan? Remember how one day the bank president himself came over to the house and signed the loan papers, no questions asked?'

'I see,' he said. 'So, when was number two?'

'Well, remember when you had that last heart attack and you needed that very tricky operation, and no surgeon would touch you? Remember how Dr. Smith came all the way up here to do the surgery himself?'

'I love that you should do such a thing for me – to save my life! I couldn't have a more wonderful wife. When was number 3?'

'Well, remember a few years ago when you really wanted to be president of the golf club and you were 17 votes short?'

Birthday gift:

A couple have not been getting along for years, so the husband thinks, 'I'll buy my wife a cemetery plot for her birthday.'

So, you can imagine her disappointment. The next year, her birthday rolled around again and this time he didn't get her anything so she asks, 'Why didn't you get me a birthday present this year?'

He sighs and replies, 'You didn't use the one I gave you last year!'

Her Well-Kept Secret:

A man and woman had been married for more than 60 years. They had shared everything. They had talked about everything. They had kept no secrets from each other except that the little old woman had a locked chest on top of her closet that she had cautioned her husband never to open or ask her about.

For all of these years, he had never thought about the chest, but one day the little old woman got very sick and the doctor said she would not recover.

In trying to sort out their affairs, the little old man took down the chest and took it to his wife's bedside. She agreed that it was time that he should know what was in the chest. When he opened it, he found two crocheted dolls and a stack of money totalling $95,000.

He asked her about the contents.

'When we were to be married,' she said, 'my grandmother told me the secret of a happy marriage was to never argue. She told me that if I ever got angry with you, I should just keep quiet and crochet a doll.'

The little old man was so moved; he had to fight back tears. Only two precious dolls were in the chest. She had only been angry with him two times in all those years of living and loving. He almost burst with happiness.

'Honey,' he said, 'that explains these two dolls, but what about all of this money? Where did it come from?'

'Oh,' she said, 'that's the money I made from selling the other dolls.'

The castle:

I made my girlfriend's dreams come true by marrying her in a castle. You wouldn't have thought she was pleased though, when I noticed the miserable look on her face as we were bouncing around!'

Japanese sex:

A Japanese couple is arguing about how to perform highly erotic sex.

Husband: 'Sukitaki. Mojitaka!'

Wife replies: 'Kowanini! Mowi janakpa!'

Husband says angrily: 'Toka a anji rodi roumi yakoo!'

Wife on her knees, literally begging: 'Mimi Nakoundinda tinkouji!'

Husband shouts angrily: 'Na miaou kina Tim kouji!'

I can't believe you just sat there trying to read this! You don't know any Japanese! You'll read anything as long as it's about sex... Sometimes I worry about you. You're in need of serious help.

The disco:

I took the other half to a disco last night. There was a bloke on the dance floor dancing up a storm, break dancing, back flips, moonwalking – the works. The other half said, 'That guy proposed to me twenty years ago and I turned him down.'

I replied, 'Looks like he's still celebrating.'

Old negative:

A wife was curious when she found an old negative in a drawer and had it made into a print. She was pleasantly surprised to see that they were of her at a much younger, slimmer time, taken many years ago on one of her first dates with her husband. When she showed him the photo, his face lit up. 'Wow, look at that!' he said with appreciation, 'That's my old Ford!'

Deporting seniors:

To help save the economy, the government will announce next month that the Immigration Department will start deporting senior citizens (instead of illegals) in order to lower pensions and healthcare costs (flu jabs, walkers, wheelchairs, free prescriptions, bus passes).

The government has established that older people are easier to catch and in most cases, will not remember how to get back home. I started to cry when I thought of you – maybe I would never see you again. Then it dawned on me... I'll see you on the bus!

He's too hot:

Wife, 'Leave me alone!'
Husband, 'It won't take long.'
Wife, 'I won't be able to sleep afterwards.'
Husband, 'I can't sleep without it.'
Wife, 'Why do you think of things like this in the middle of the night?'
Husband, 'Because I'm hot.'
Wife, 'You get hot at the darnedest times.'
Husband, 'If you loved me, I wouldn't have to beg you.'
Wife, 'If you loved me, you'd be more considerate.'
Husband, 'You don't love me any more.'
Wife, 'Yes I do, but let's forget it for tonight.'
Husband, 'Please... go on'
Wife, 'All right. I'll do it.'
Husband, 'What's the matter? You need a flashlight?'
Wife, 'I can't find it in the dark.'
Husband, 'Oh, for heaven's sake – feel for it!'
Wife, 'There! Are you satisfied?'
Husband, 'Oh, yes.'
Wife, 'Is it up far enough?'
Wife, 'Yeah, that's good.
Wife, 'Right! Now go to sleep, and the next time you want the bloody window open, do it yourself.'

Now what were you expecting??

The Mercedes

A senior couple returned to a Mercedes dealership where the salesman had just sold the car they were interested in to a beautiful, leggy, busty blonde.

'I thought you said you would hold that car till we raised the $75,000 asking price,' said the man. 'Yet, I just heard you close the deal for $65,000 to the lovely young lady there. You insisted to us that there could be no discount on this model.'

'Well, what can I tell you? She had the ready cash and just look at her, how could I resist?' replied the grinning salesman.

Just then the young woman approached the elderly gentleman and gave them the keys. 'There you go,' she said, 'I told you I would get the dope to reduce it. See you later grandad.'

Don't mess with seniors!

The funeral:

A funeral procession pulled into a cemetery. Several carloads of family members followed a black truck towing a boat with a coffin in it.

A passer-by remarked, 'That guy must have been a very avid fisherman.'

'Oh, he still is,' remarked one of the mourners. As a matter of fact, he's heading off to the lake as soon as we bury his wife.'

The escapee:

A man escapes from prison where he has been for 15 years. He breaks into a house to look for money and guns, and finds a young couple in bed. He orders the guy out of bed and ties him to a chair. He ties the girl to the bed and he gets on top of her, kisses her neck, and then gets up and goes into the bathroom.

While he's in there, the husband tells his wife: 'Listen, this guy is an escaped convict, look at his clothes! He probably spent lots of time in jail and hasn't seen a woman in years. I saw how he kissed your neck. If he wants sex, don't resist, don't complain, do whatever he tells you. Satisfy him no matter how much he nauseates you. This guy is probably very dangerous. If he gets angry, he'll kill us. Be strong, honey. I love you.'

His wife responds: 'He wasn't kissing my neck. He was whispering in my ear. He told me he was gay, thought you were cute, and asked me if we had any Vaseline. I told him it was in the bathroom. Be strong honey. I love you, too!'

Flying a Kite:

I was in my back yard trying to launch a kite. I threw the kite up in the air, the wind would catch it for a few seconds, then it would come crashing back down to earth. I tried this a few more times with no success.

All the while, my wife Jan was watching from the kitchen window, muttering to herself how men need to be told everything. She opened the window and yelled at me, 'You need a piece of tail.'

I turned with a confused look on my face and said, 'Make up your mind. Last night you told me to go fly a kite.'

Love your husband:

A group of women were at a seminar on how to live in a loving relationship with their husband.

The women were asked, 'How many of you love your husband?' All the women raised their hands.

Then they were asked, 'When was the last time you told your husband you loved him?'

Some women answered today, a few said yesterday, and some can't remember.

The women were then told to take out their cell phones and text to their husband: 'I love you, sweetheart.'

Then they were instructed to exchange phones with another person, and to read aloud the text message that was received in response to their message.

Below are 12 replies; some are hilarious.

1. Who the hell is this?
2. Eh, mother of my children, are you sick or what?
3. Yeah, and I love you too. What's wrong?
4. What now? Did you crash the car again?
5. I don't understand what you mean?
6. What the hell did you do now?
8. Don't beat about the bush, just tell me how much you need?
9. Am I dreaming?
10. If you don't tell me who this message is actually for, someone will die.
11. I thought we agreed you wouldn't drink during the day.
12. Your mother is coming to stay with us, isn't she?

Valentines Poem:

- My darling, my lover, my beautiful wife; marrying you has screwed up my life.
- I see your face when I'm dreaming – that's why I always wake up screaming.
- Kind, intelligent loving and hot – this describes everything you are not.
- I thought that I could love no other, that is until I met your brother.
- I want to feel your sweet embrace, but don't take that paper bag off your face.
- I love your smile, your face and your eyes – damn I'm good at telling lies!

- My love, you take my breath away – what have you stepped in to smell this way?
- What inspired the amorous rhyme? Two parts vodka and one-part lime.

Who said poetry is dead.

A married man's prayer:

Dear God, 'You gave me childhood, you took it away; you gave me youth, you took it away; you gave me a wife... It's been twenty years now, just reminding you.'

Trivia:

- A man gave his wife a diamond necklace for their anniversary and his wife didn't speak to him for six months.
  Friend: 'Why? Was the necklace a fake?'
  'Nooooo... That was our deal.'

- A couple was having dinner at a fancy restaurant. As the food was served, the husband said, 'The food looks delicious; let's eat.'
  Wife: 'Honey, you say a prayer before eating at home.'
  Husband: 'That's at home sweetheart. Here the chef knows how to cook.'

- Employee:' Sir, you're like a lion in the office. What about at home?'
  Boss: 'I'm a lion at home too, but there we have a lion tamer.'

Questions and Answers:

Q. What four words are the worst that a woman can say to a man?
A. Is it in yet?

Q. From where do you get steel wool?
A. Shearing hydraulic rams.

Q: How does a physicist exercise?

A: By pumping ion!

Q: Why does someone who runs marathons make a good student?
A: Because education pays off in the long run!

Q: What's the difference between Big Foot and an intelligent man?
A: Big Foot's been spotted several times.

Q: What do you get when you cross a snake and a kangaroo?
A: A jump rope!

Q: What kind of horses go out after dusk?
A: Nightmares!

Q: What do you get when you cross a frog with a rabbit?
A: A Bunny Ribbit!

Q: What is smarter than a talking bird?
A: A spelling bee!

Q: What do you get when you cross a dog with a phone?
A: A golden receiver!

Q. Here's one Why do milking chairs only have three legs????
A. Because the cow has the UDDER

Q: What do you get if you cross a cocker spaniel, a poodle and a rooster?
A: Cockerpoodledoo!

Q: Why do dogs run in circles?
A: Because it's hard to run in squares!

Q: What does a television have in common with a rabbit?
A: His ears!

Q: What did the crop say to the farmer?
A: Why are you always picking on me?

CHAPTER 4

POLITICS

Political one-liners:

- When they call the roll in the Senate, the Senators don't know whether to answer 'present' or 'not guilty.'
- Why pay money to have your family tree traced; go into politics and your opponents will do it for you.
- Politicians are people who, when they see light at the end of the tunnel, go out and buy some more tunnel.
- Politics is the gentle art of getting votes from the poor and campaign funds from the rich, by promising to protect each from the other.
- Suppose you were an idiot. And suppose you were a member of government. But then I repeat myself.
- I have come to the conclusion that politics is too serious a matter to be left to the politicians.
- There ought to be one day – just one – when there is open season on politicians.
- The word politics is derived from the word poly, meaning many and the word ticks, meaning blood sucking parasites.
- Ineptocracy – a system of government where the least capable to lead are elected by the least capable of producing, and where the members of society least likely to sustain themselves or succeed, are rewarded with goods and services paid for by the confiscated wealth of a diminishing number of producers.
- What happens if a politician drowns in a river?" It's pollution. What happens if all of them drown? That's a solution.
- No man's life, liberty or property is safe while parliament is in session.
- There is no distinctly criminal class save government.

- I contend that for a nation to try to tax itself into prosperity is like a man standing in a bucket and trying to lift himself up by the handle.
- If God wanted us to vote, he would have given us candidates.
- In my many years, I have come to the conclusion that one useless man is a shame, two is a law firm and three or more is a government.
- A politician is a fellow who will lay down *your* life for his country.
- Don't blame politicians for disappointing you, blame yourself for expecting too much from them.
- I think Politicians should wear uniforms, you know, like racing drivers, so we can identify their corporate sponsors.
- Foreign aid might be defined as a transfer of money from poor people in rich countries to rich people in poor countries.
- We hang the petty thieves and appoint the great ones to public office.
- Politicians should have two terms – one in office and another in prison.
- Government plan big things for tomorrow in spite of zero knowledge of the future.
- The government is like a baby's alimentary canal, with a happy appetite at one end and no responsibility at the other.
- I hope they never find life on any other planet, because sure as hell, our government will start sending them money.
- When I was a boy, I was told that anybody could become Prime Minister, and I'm beginning to believe it.
- Politicians are the same all over. They promise to build a bridge even where there is no river.

- The problems we face today are there because the people who work for a living are outnumbered by those who vote for a living.

Oldie but goodie:

Cicero, 55 BC

The budget should be balanced, the treasury would be refilled, public debt should be reduced, the arrogance of officialdom should be tempered and controlled and the assistance to foreign lands should be curtailed, lest Rome will become bankrupt. People must again learn to work instead of living on public assistance.

So, evidently we've learned bugger all over the past 2,071 years!

The gangster:

After a thorough investigation, a rich gangster finds out that his bookkeeper has cheated him out of ten million bucks. His bookkeeper is deaf and that was the reason he got the job in the first place. It was assumed that a deaf bookkeeper would not hear anything that he might have to testify about in court.

When the mobster goes to confront the bookkeeper about his missing $10 million, he brings along his attorney, who knows sign language.

The Godfather tells the lawyer, 'Ask him where the $10 million bucks he embezzled from me is.'

The attorney, using sign language, asks the bookkeeper: 'Where is the money?'

The bookkeeper signs back: 'I don't know what you are talking about.'

The attorney tells the gangster: 'He says he doesn't know what you're talking about.'

The gangster pulls out a pistol, puts it to the bookkeeper's temple and says, 'Ask him again!'

The attorney signs to the bookkeeper: 'He'll kill you if you don't tell him!'

The bookkeeper signs back: 'Okay! Okay! You win! The money is in a brown briefcase, buried behind the shed in my cousin Enzo's backyard in Queens!'

The Godfather asks the attorney: 'Well, what'd he say?'

'He says you don't have the guts to pull the trigger.'

Today's lesson in irony:

The food stamp program is administered by the US Department of Agriculture. They proudly report that they distribute free meals and food stamps to over 46 million people on an annual basis.

Meanwhile, the National Park Service, run by the US Department of the Interior, asks us, 'Please do not feed the animals.'

And their stated reason for this policy? 'The animals will grow dependent on the handouts and then they will never learn how to take care of themselves.'

That concludes today's lesson.

Best education:

Remember: most politicians are lawyers.

A father told his three sons when he sent them to the university: 'I feel it's my duty to provide you with the best possible education, and you do not owe me anything for that. However, I want you to appreciate it; as a token, please each put $1,000 into my coffin when I die.'

And so it happened. The sons became a doctor, a lawyer, and a financial planner, each very successful financially.

When they saw their father in the coffin one day, they remembered his wish.

First it was the doctor who put ten $100 bills into the coffin of the deceased.

Then came the financial planner, who put a $1,000 bill there, too.

Finally, it was the heartbroken lawyer's turn. He dipped into his pocket, took out his cheque book, wrote a check for $3,000, put it into his father's coffin, and took the $2,000 cash. The lawyer later went on to become a member of Parliament.

The Genie:

A man was walking along a Vancouver beach when he came across a lamp partially buried in the sand. He picked up the lamp and gave it a rub. A genie appeared and told him he will be granted one wish.

The man thinks for a moment and says, 'I want to live forever.'

'Sorry,' said the genie, 'I'm not allowed to grant eternal life.'

'Okay then, I want to die after the parliament balance the budget and eliminate the debt.'

'You crafty little bastard,' said the genie.

Canadian National Anthem:

When CBC had a pole and asked the question, 'Do you believe that the word 'God' should stay in the iconic National Anthem ... a part of Canadian culture?' they had the highest number of responses that they have ever had for one of their polls, and the percentage was this: 86% for the words "God keep our Land, in the National Anthem, 14% against. That is a pretty commanding public response.

Because 86% of Canadians believe the word 'God' should stay, why is there such a controversy about having the word 'God' in the anthem. Should the country cater to the 14% who don't? I don't think so!

The Canadian National Anthem:

Oh Canada, our home and native land.
True patriot love in all our sons command.
With glowing hearts, we see thee rise.
The true north strong and free.
From far and wide oh Canada.
We stand on guard for thee.
GOD keep our land glorious and free.
Oh Canada we stand on guard for thee.
Oh Canada we stand on guard for thee.

Harley Biker:

A Harley Biker is riding by the zoo in Washington, DC when he sees a little girl leaning into the lion's cage. Suddenly, the lion grabs her by the collar of her jacket and tries to pull her inside to slaughter her, under the eyes of her screaming parents. The biker jumps off his Harley, runs to the cage and hits the lion square on the nose with a powerful punch. Whimpering from the pain the lion jumps back letting go of the girl, and the biker brings the girl to her terrified parents, who thank him endlessly. A reporter has watched the whole event.

The reporter addressing the Harley rider says, 'Sir, this was the most gallant and bravest thing I've seen a man do in my whole life.'

The Harley rider replies, 'Why, it was nothing, really. The lion was behind bars. I just saw this little kid in danger, and acted as I felt right.'

The reporter says, 'Well, I'll make sure this won't go unnoticed. I'm a journalist, you know, and tomorrow's paper will have this story on the front page. So, what do you do for a living, and what political affiliation do you have?'

The biker replies 'I'm a U.S. Marine, a Republican and I'm voting for Trump.' The journalist leaves.

The following morning the biker buys the paper to see if it indeed brings news of his actions, and reads, on the front page: ***U.S. marine assaults African immigrant and steals his lunch.***

And THAT pretty much sums up the media's approach to the news these days!

Historical fact:

Who says building a border wall won't work? The Chinese built one over 2,000 years ago and they still don't have any Mexicans.

Removing phones:

The government of China announced today that they would be removing all telephones from their country. After six months of hard lobbying, the organisation for independent speech convinced the Chinese politicians to take action who argued there were too many Wings and Wongs and that many people were becoming annoyed when others Wing the Wong number.

Employee notice for old people:

Due to the current financial situation caused by the slowdown in the economy, the Government has decided to implement a scheme to put workers of 50 years of age and above on early mandatory retirement, this creating jobs and reducing unemployment.

This scheme will be known as RAPE (Retire Aged People Early). Persons selected to be RAPED can apply to the Government to be considered for the SHAFT program (Special Help After Forced Termination).

Persons who have been RAPED and SHAFTED will be reviewed under the SCREW program (System Covering Retired Early Workers). A person may be RAPED once, SHAFTED twice and SCREWED as many times as the Government deems appropriate.

Persons who have been RAPED could get AIDS (Additional Income for Dependents and Spouse) or HERPES (Half Earnings for Retired Personnel Early Severance).

Obviously, persons who have AIDS or HERPES will not be SHAFTED or SCREWED any further by the Government. Persons who are not RAPED and are staying on, will receive as much SHIT (Special High Intensity Training) as possible. The Government has always prided themselves on the amount of SHIT they give our citizens.

Should you feel that you do not receive enough SHIT, please bring this to the attention of your MP, who has been trained to give you all the SHIT you can handle.

Sincerely,

The Committee for Economic Value of Individual Lives (EVIL).

PS – Due to recent budget cuts and the rising cost of electricity, gas and oil, as well as current market conditions, the Light at the End of the Tunnel has been turned off.

Salt and pepper:

There was a luncheon for newly sworn in politicians. When they sat down, one of them discovered that their salt shaker contained pepper and their pepper shaker was full of salt. How could they swap the contents of the two without spilling any and using only the implements at hand.

Clearly, this was a job for bright minds. The group debated the problem and presented ideas and finally came up with a brilliant solution involving a napkin, a straw and an empty saucer. They called the waitress over, ready to dazzle her with their solution.

'Miss,' they said, 'we couldn't help but notice that the pepper shaker contains salt and the salt shaker has pepper.'

But before they could finish, the waitress interrupted. 'Oh, sorry about that.'

She leaned over the table, unscrewed the caps of both shakers and switched them. There was dead silence at the table.

Sick prime minister:

The Prime Minister had to spend a couple of days in the hospital. He was a major nuisance to the nurses because he bossed them around just like he did his ministers. None of the hospital staff wanted to have anything to do with him. The head nurse was the only one who could stand up to him. She came into his room and announced, 'I have to take your temperature.'

After complaining for several minutes, he finally settled down, crossed his arms and opened his mouth.

'No, I'm sorry,' the nurse stated, 'but for this reading, I can't use an oral thermometer.'

This started another round of complaining, but eventually he rolled over and bared his rear end.

After feeling the nurse insert the thermometer, he heard her announce, 'I have to get something Now you stay just like that till I get back.'

He leaves the door to his room open on her way out. He curses under his breath as he hears people walking past his door laughing.

After almost half an hour, his doctor comes into the room.

'What's going on here?' he asks.

Angrily the Prime Minister answers, 'What's the matter, Doc? Haven't you ever seen someone having their temperature taken?'

After a pause, the doctor confesses, 'Not with a sunflower.'

Best patients:

Five surgeons discuss who makes the best patients to operate on.

- The first surgeon says, 'I like to see accountants on my operating table because when you open them up, everything inside is numbered.'
- The second responds, 'Yeah, but you should try electricians! Everything inside them is colour coded.'
- The third surgeon says, 'No, I really think librarians are the best! Everything inside them is in alphabetical order.'
- The fourth surgeon chimes in, 'You know, I like construction workers. Those guys always understand when you have a few parts left over.'
- But the fifth surgeon, shut them all up when he said, 'You're all wrong. Politicians are the easiest to operate on. There's no guts, no heart, no balls, no brains and no spine – plus the head and the arse are interchangeable!'

At the bar:

Having already downed a few power drinks, she turns around, faces him, looks him straight in the eye and says, 'Listen here good looking, I screw anybody, anytime, anywhere, your place, my place, in the car, front door, back door, on the ground, standing up, sitting down, naked or with clothes on, dirty, clean, it doesn't matter to me. I've been doing it ever since I got out of college and I just love it.'

Eyes now wide with interest, he responds, 'No kidding. I'm a lawyer too. What firm are you with?'

Butch the Rooster:

Sarah was in the fertilized egg business. She had several hundred young pullets and ten roosters to fertilize the eggs. She kept records and any rooster not performing went into the soup pot and was replaced.

This took a lot of time, so she bought some tiny bells and attached them to her roosters. Each bell had a different ring to it, so she could tell from a distance which rooster was performing. Now, she could sit on the porch and fill out an efficiency report by just listening to the bells.

Sarah's favourite rooster, old Butch, was a very fine specimen but, this morning she noticed old Butch's bell hadn't rung at all! When she went to investigate, she saw the other roosters were busy chasing pullets, bells-a-ringing, but the pullets hearing the roosters coming, would run for cover.

To Sarah's amazement, old Butch had his bell in his beak, so it couldn't ring. He'd sneak up on a pullet, do his job, and walk on to the next one. Sarah was so proud of old Butch, she entered him in a Show and he became an overnight sensation among the judges.

The result was the judges not only awarded old Butch the 'No Bell Peace Prize' they also awarded him the 'Pullet Surprise' as well.

Clearly old Butch was a politician in the making. Who else but a politician could figure out how to win two of the most coveted awards on our planet by being the best at sneaking up on the unsuspecting populace and screwing them when they weren't paying attention? Vote carefully in the next election. You can't always hear the bells.

Famous quotes:

In my many years I have come to a conclusion that one useless man is a shame, two is a law firm and three or more is a government. **John Adams.**

If you don't read the newspaper you are uninformed, if you do read the newspaper you are misinformed. *(how true is that!!!)* **Mark Twain.**

Suppose you were an idiot. And suppose you were a member of government. But then I repeat myself. **Mark Twain.**

I contend that for a nation to try to tax itself into prosperity is like a man standing in a bucket and trying to lift himself up by the handle. **Winston Churchill.**

A government which robs Peter to pay Paul can always depend on the support of Paul. **George Bernard Shaw.**

Foreign aid might be defined as a transfer of money from poor people in rich countries to rich people in poor countries. **Douglas Casey,** Classmate of Bill Clinton at Georgetown University.

Giving money and power to government is like giving whiskey and car keys to teenage boys. **P.J. O'Rourke,** Civil Libertarian.

Government is the great fiction, through which everybody endeavours to live at the expense of everybody else. **Frederic Bastiat,** French economist (1801-1850)

I don't make jokes. I just watch the government and report the facts. **Will Rogers.**

If you think health care is expensive now, wait until you see what it costs when it's free! **P.J. O'Rourke.**

In general, the art of government consists of taking as much money as possible from one party of the citizens to give to the other. **Voltaire (1764.)**

Just because you do not take an interest in politics doesn't mean politics won't take an interest in you! **Pericles (430 B.C.)**

No man's life, liberty, or property is safe while the legislature is in session **Mark Twain (1866)**

Talk is cheap... except when government does it. **Anonymous**

The government is like a baby's alimentary canal, with a happy appetite at one end and no responsibility at the other. **Ronald Reagan.**

The only difference between a tax man and a taxidermist is that the taxidermist leaves the skin. **Mark Twain.**

What this country needs are more unemployed politicians. **Edward Langley,** Artist (1928-1995.)

A government big enough to give you everything you want, is strong enough to take everything you have. **Thomas Jefferson.**

We hang the petty thieves and appoint the great ones to public office. **Aesop.**

'Police in Australia are searching for a group of men seen releasing live crocodiles into a school building. Though, if you ask me, they should probably be searching for the crocodiles.' **Seth Meyers.**

Husbands are like fires - they go out when unattended. – **Zsa Zsa Gabor**

Snotty receptionist:

An older gentleman had an appointment to see the urologist who shared offices with several other doctors. The waiting room was filled with patients. As he approached the receptionist's desk he noticed that the receptionist was a large unfriendly woman who looked like a Sumo wrestler. He gave her his name and in a very loud voice she said, 'Yes, I have your name here. You want to see the doctor about impotence, right?'

All the patients in the waiting room snapped their heads around to look at the very embarrassed man. He recovered quickly and in an equally loud voice replied, 'No I've come to enquire about a sex change operation, but I don't want the same doctor that did yours.'

Don't mess with old folks!

Complaint

A woman, Mrs. Maynard, has sued a hospital saying that after her husband had surgery there he lost all interest in sex. A hospital spokesman replied: 'Mr. Maynard was admitted for cataract surgery. All we did was correct his eyesight.'

Older patient:

Nurse to older man, 'The doctor would like a stool, urine and sperm sample.'
Man with hand to his ear, 'What did she say?'
Wife, 'They want your underwear.'

The vasectomy:

After a check-up, a doctor asked his patient:
'Is there anything you'd like to discuss?'
'Well,' said the patient, 'I was thinking about getting a vasectomy.'
'That's a big decision. Have you talked it over with your family?'
'Yes, we took a vote – and they're in favour of it 15 to 2.'

Weight loss excuses:

1. I have metal fillings in my teeth. My fridge magnets keep pulling me into the kitchen. That's why I can't lose weight.'
2. Doctor: 'What fits your busy schedule better – exercising one hour a day or being dead 24 hours a day?'
3. Woman to waiter: 'I'm going to order a broiled skinless chicken breast, but I want you to bring me lasagne and garlic bread by mistake.'

4. 'If I put a crouton on my sundae instead of a cherry – it counts as being a salad.'
5. Doctor to patient: 'Pulling the handle on the recliner chair does not qualify as part of an exercise plan.'
6. 'My toes voted and decided they didn't want to go jogging today.'
7. 'Donut holes have no calories, however, you have to eat the rest of the donut to get to it.'
8. Sign on concrete block: Exercise Block
   Place block on the floor
   Walk around it twice.
   Sit down and relax!
   You've just walked around the block twice – aren't you proud?

Walking can add minutes to your life.

- This enables you at 85 years old to spend an additional five months in a nursing home at $7,000 per month.
- My dad started walking five miles a day when he was 60. Now he's 105 years old, and we don't have the slightest clue where he is.
- I like long walks, especially when they are taken by people who annoy me.
- The only reason I would take up walking, is so that I could hear heavy breathing again.
- I have to walk early in the morning, before my brain figures out what I'm doing.
- I joined a Wellness Centre last year, spent over 700 bucks - haven't lost a pound. Apparently you have to go there.
- Every time I hear the dirty word 'exercise', I wash my mouth out with chocolate.
- The advantage of exercising every day is so when you die, they'll say, 'Well, he looks good doesn't he'! (One of the three stages of man - childhood, adulthood and he looks good!)

- If you are going to try cross-country skiing, start with a small country.
- I know I got a lot of exercise the last few years just getting over the hill.
- We all get heavier as we get older, because there's a lot more information in our heads. That's my story and I'm sticking to it. And...
- Every time I start thinking too much about how I look, I just find a Happy Hour and by the time I leave, I look just fine.

Hurt bad:

Late in the night, Jim, a Corporal Mine Defuser, finally regained consciousness. He was in a Field Evacuation Hospital, in agonizing pain. He found himself in the ICU with tubes in his mouth, needles and IV drips in both arms, a breathing mask, wires monitoring every function and a gorgeous nurse hovering over him.

He realized that he was obviously in a life-threatening situation. The nurse gave him a serious deep look straight into his eyes then spoke to him slowly and clearly, enunciating each word and syllable, 'You may not feel anything from the waist down.'

Also speaking slowly, he managed to mumble a reply, 'Can I feel your tits, then?'

And that, friends, is a Positive Attitude!

Four-letter word:

A man is recovering from surgery when the surgical nurse appears and asks him how he is feeling.

'I'm okay, but I didn't like the four-letter word the doctor used in surgery,' he answered.

'What did he say?' asked the nurse.

'Oops!'

The check-up:

Doctor: 'Your lab tests show that you're doing fairly well for a 65-year-old.'
Patient: 'Fairly well! Do you think I'll live to be 80?'
Doctor: Do you smoke tobacco or drink beer or wine?
Patient: 'No. I'm not doing drugs either.'
Doctor: 'Do you eat ribeye steaks or barbecued ribs?'
Patient: 'No. I think all red meat is very unhealthy.'
Doctor: Do you spend a lot of time in the sun like golfing, sailing, fishing, hiking or bicycling?'
Patient: 'No, I don't.'
Doctor: 'Do you gamble, drive fast cars or have a lot of sex?'
Patient: 'No. I don't do any of those things.'
Doctor: 'Then why the hell do you want to live to be 80?'

Flu season:

Take the doctor's approach to dealing with the flu. Think about it... When you go in for a flu jab, what do they do first? They clean your arm with alcohol.

Why? Because alcohol kills germs.

So, I walk to the pub (exercise); I put lime in my vodka (fruit); celery in my Bloody Mary (veggies); drink outdoors on the patio (fresh air); tell jokes and laugh (eliminate stress); then I pass out (rest). The way I see it, if you keep your alcohol levels up, flu germs can't get you.

Remember: A shot in the glass is better than one in the arse.

Fluid on the knee:

I went to the doctor with fluid on the knee and he advised, 'You're not aiming right.'

His libido

An Irish woman of advanced age visited her physician to ask his advice in reviving her husband's libido.

'What about trying Viagra?' asked the doctor.

'Not a chance', she said. 'He won't even take an aspirin.'

'Not a problem,' replied the doctor. 'Give him an 'Irish Viagra'. It's when you drop the Viagra tablet into his coffee. He won't even taste it. Give it a try and call me in a week to let me know how things go.'

It wasn't a week later when she called the doctor, who directly inquired as to her progress. The poor dear exclaimed, 'Oh, faith, bejaysus and begorrah! T'was horrid! Just terrible, doctor!

'Really? What happened?' asked the doctor.

'Well, I did as you advised and slipped it in his coffee and the effect was almost immediate. He jumped straight up, with a twinkle in his eye and with his pants a-bulging fiercely! With one swoop of his arm, he sent me cups and tablecloth flying, ripped me clothes to tatters and took me then and there passionately on the tabletop! It was a nightmare, I tell you, an absolute nightmare!'

'Why so terrible?' asked the doctor, 'Do you mean the sex your husband provided wasn't good?'

'Feckin jaysus, 'twas the best sex I've had in twenty-five years! But sure as I'm sittin here, I'll never be able to show me face in that coffee shop again.

Mail order catalogue:

Two Irishmen were looking at a mail order catalogue and admiring the models. One said to the other, 'Have you seen the beautiful girls in this catalogue?'

The second one replies, 'Yes, they are very beautiful.

And look at the price!' The first one says, with wide eyes, 'Wow, they aren't very expensive. At this price, I'm buying one.'

The second one smiles and pats him on the back. 'Good idea! Order one and if she's as beautiful as she is in the catalogue, I will get one too.'

Three weeks later, the youngest Irishman asks his pal, 'Did you ever receive the girl you ordered from the catalogue?'

The second Irishman replies, 'No, but it shouldn't be long now. All her clothes arrived yesterday!!'

Black Testicles:

A male patient is lying in bed in the hospital, wearing an oxygen mask over his mouth and nose.

A young student nurse appears and gives him a partial sponge bath.

'Nurse,' he mumbles from behind the mask, 'are my testicles black?'

Embarrassed, the young nurse replies, 'I don't know, Sir. I'm only here to wash your upper body and feet.'

He struggles to ask again, 'Nurse, please check for me. Are my testicles black?'

Concerned that he might elevate his blood pressure and heart rate from worrying about his testicles, she overcomes her embarrassment and pulls back the covers.

She raises his gown, holds his manhood in one hand and his testicles gently in the other.

She looks very closely and says, 'There's nothing wrong with them, Sir. They look magnificent.'

The man slowly pulls off his oxygen mask, smiles at her, and says very slowly, 'Thank you very much. That was wonderful. Now listen very, very closely: 'Are - My - Test - Results - Back?'

The colonoscopy:

Being nervous, and embarrassed about my upcoming colonoscopy, on a recommendation I decided to have it done while visiting friends in San Francisco, where the beautiful nurses are allegedly more gentle and accommodating.

As I lay naked on my side on the table, the gorgeous nurse began my procedure.

'Don't worry, at this stage of the procedure; it's quite normal to get an erection,' the nurse told me.

'I haven't got an erection,' I replied.

'No, but I have,' replied the nurse.

Don't get a colonoscopy in San Francisco.

Not well:

This is what all of us: 70+, other seniors, and kids (south of 60) have to look forward to!! This is something that happened at an assisted living center.

The people who lived there have small apartments but they all eat at a central cafeteria. One morning one of the residents didn't show up for breakfast so my wife went upstairs and knocked on his door to see if everything was okay. She could hear him through the door and he said that he was running late and would be down shortly so she went back to the dining area.

An hour later he still hadn't arrived so she went back up towards his room and she found him on the stairs. He was coming down the stairs but was having a hell of time. He had a death grip on the hand rail and seemed to have trouble getting his legs to work right. She told him she was going to call an ambulance but he told her no, he wasn't in any pain and just wanted to have his breakfast. So she helped him the rest of the way down the stairs and he had his breakfast.

When he tried to return to his room he was completely unable to get up even the first step so they called an ambulance for him. A couple hours later she called the hospital to see how he was doing. The receptionist there said he was fine, he just had both of his legs in one leg of his boxer shorts.

The hokey pokey clinic:

A place to turn yourself around.

Engineer in Hell:

An Engineer dies and goes to Hell. Dissatisfied with the level of comfort, he starts designing and building improvements. After a while, Hell has air conditioning, flush toilets and escalators. The engineer is a pretty popular guy.

One day, God calls and asks Satan, 'So, how's it going down there?' Satan says, 'Hey things are going great. We've got air conditioning and flush toilets and escalators and there's no telling what this engineer is going to come up with next.'

God is horrified. 'What? You've got an engineer? That's a mistake; he should never have gone down there! You know all engineers go to Heaven. Send him up here!'

Satan says, 'No way. I like having an engineer on the staff. I'm keeping him.'

God says, 'Send him back up here, or I'll sue.'

'Yeah, right,' Satan laughs, 'and where are you going to get a lawyer from?

Reason for visit:

Suspecting he had a serious medical condition, I nagged my husband until he agreed to see a doctor. Once there, he was handed a mountain of forms to fill out.

Next to "Reason for visit?" he wrote, 'My wife made me.'

For your legal knowledge:

Sounds gruesome but it is a fact!

In old Roman Courts, instead of taking oath on the sacred books, men used to swear holding their testicles. Hence the word 'testify' originated from the word 'testicles'. If proven false, the testes of liars were cut and fed to the dogs tied nearby. [Yuch]

(This punitive action could be very effective even today, especially for many politicians in power!)

Female Justice:

Here is her story in her own words:

'While out walking along the edge of a pond just outside of The Villages with my soon-to-be ex-husband discussing property settlement and other divorce issues, we were surprised by a huge 12-ft. alligator which suddenly emerged from the murky water and began charging us with its large jaws wide open. She must have been protecting her nest because she was extremely aggressive.

If I had not had my little Beretta JetFire .25 calibre pistol with me, I would not be here today! Just one shot to my estranged husband's knee cap was all it took. The 'gator got him easily and I was able to escape by just walking away at a brisk pace. It's one of the best pistols in my collection! Plus the amount I saved in lawyer's fees was really incredible!'

CHAPTER 5

DOCTORS

Diagnosis:

A bloke went to his doctor and told him that he's having trouble doing things around his home that he used to do without trouble. When the examination was complete he asked, 'Doc, tell me in plain English – what's wrong with me?'

'Well in plain English,' the doctor replied, 'you're just lazy.'

'Okay,' nodded the man. 'Now give me the medical term so I can tell my wife.'

19 ways to live instead of exist:

Some of us have reached our golden years, and some of us have not. But these suggestions should be read by everyone! They've been collected from many a senior, each with his or her own piece of advice. Some you know, some may surprise you, and some will remind you of what's important. So read well, share with your loved ones, and have a great day and a great life!

Don't be afraid of death – be afraid of an unlived life. You don't have to live forever – you just have to live – not exist.

The trouble is – you think you have time. I'd rather look back at my life and say, 'I can't believe I did that' instead of saying 'I wish I'd done that.'

1. It's time to use the money you saved up. Use it and enjoy it. Don't just keep it for those who may have no notion of the sacrifices you made to get it. Remember there is nothing more dangerous than a son or daughter-in-law with big ideas for your hard earned capital. Warning: This is also a bad time for an investment, even if it seems wonderful or fool-proof. They only bring

problems and worries and this is a time for you to enjoy some peace and quiet.
2. Stop worrying about the financial situation of your children and grandchildren, and don't feel bad spending your money on yourself. You've taken care of them for many years, and you've taught them what you could. You gave them an education, food, shelter and support. The responsibility is now theirs to earn their own money.
3. Keep a healthy life, without great physical effort. Do moderate exercise (like walking every day), eat well and get your sleep. It's easy to become sick, and it gets harder to remain healthy. That is why you need to keep yourself in good shape and be aware of your medical and physical needs. Keep in touch with your doctor, get tested even when you're feeling well. Stay informed.
4. Always buy the best, most beautiful items for your significant other. The key goal is to enjoy your money with your partner. One day one of you will miss the other, and the money will not provide any comfort then, enjoy it together.
5. Don't stress over the little things. You've already overcome so much in your life. You have good memories and bad ones, but the important thing is the present. Don't let the past drag you down and don't let the future frighten you. Feel good in the now. Small issues will soon be forgotten.
6. Regardless of age, always keep love alive. Love your partner, love life, love your family, love your neighbour and remember: 'A man is not old as long as he has intelligence and affection.'
7. Be proud, both inside and out. Don't stop going to your hair salon or barber, do your nails, go to the dermatologist and the dentist, keep your perfumes and creams well stocked. When you are well-maintained on the outside, it seeps in, making you feel proud and strong.

8. Don't lose sight of fashion trends for your age, but keep your own sense of style. There's nothing worse than an older person trying to wear the current fashion among youngsters. You've developed your own sense of what looks good on you - keep it and be proud of it. It's part of who you are.
9. Always stay up-to-date. Read newspapers, watch the news. Go online and read what people are saying. Make sure you have an active e-mail account and try to use some of those social networks. You'll be surprised which old friends you'll meet. Keeping in touch with what is going on and with the people you know is important.
10. Respect the younger generation and their opinions. They may not have the same ideals as you, but they are the future, and will take the world in their direction. Give advice, not criticism, and try to remind them of yesterday's wisdom that still applies today.
11. Never use the phrase: 'In my time.' Your time is now. As long as you're alive, you are part of this time. You may have been younger, but you are still you now; having fun and enjoying life.
12. Some people embrace their golden years, while others become bitter and surly. Life is too short to waste your days on the latter. Spend your time with positive, cheerful people, it'll rub off on you and your days will seem that much better. Spending your time with bitter people will make you older and harder to be around.
13. Do not surrender to the temptation of living with your children or grandchildren (if you have a financial choice, that is). Sure, being surrounded by family sounds great, but we all need our privacy. They need theirs and you need yours. If you've lost your partner (our deepest condolences), then find a person to move in with you and help out. Even then, do so only if you feel you really need the help or do not want to live alone.
14. Don't abandon your hobbies. If you don't have any, make new ones. You can travel, hike, cook, read, dance.

You can adopt a cat or a dog, grow a garden, play cards, checkers, chess, dominoes, golf. You can paint, volunteer at an NGO or just collect certain items. Find something you like and spend some real time having fun with it.

15. Even if you don't feel like it, try to accept invitations. Baptisms, graduations, birthdays, weddings, conferences. Try to go. Get out of the house, meet people you haven't seen in a while, experience something new (or something old). But don't get upset when you're not invited. Some events are limited by resources, and not everyone can be hosted. The important thing is to leave the house from time to time. Go to museums, go walk through a field. Get out there

16. Be a conversationalist. Talk less and listen more. Some people go on and on about the past, not caring if their listeners are really interested. That's a great way of reducing their desire to speak with you. Listen first and answer questions, but don't go off into long stories unless asked to. Speak in courteous tones and try not to complain or criticize too much unless you really need to. Try to accept situations as they are. Everyone is going through the same things, and people have a low tolerance for hearing complaints. Always find some good things to say as well.

17. Pain and discomfort go hand in hand with getting older. Try not to dwell on them but accept them as a part of the cycle of life we're all going through. Try to minimize them in your mind. They are not who you are, they are something that life added to you. If they become your entire focus, you lose sight of the person you used to be. If you have a strong belief, savour it. But don't waste your time trying to convince others. They will make their own choices no matter what you tell them, and it will only bring you frustration. Live your faith and set an example. Live true to your beliefs and let that memory sway them.

18. Laugh. Laugh A LOT. Laugh at everything. Remember, you are one of the lucky ones. You managed to have a life, a long one. Many never get to this age, never get to experience a full life. But you did. So what's not to laugh about? Find the humour in your situation.
19. Take no notice of what others say about you and even less notice of what they might be thinking. They'll do it anyway, and you should have pride in yourself and what you've achieved. Let them talk and don't worry. They have no idea about your history, your memories and the life you've lived so far. There's still much to be written, so get busy writing and don't waste time thinking about what others might think. Now is the time to be at rest, at peace and as happy as you can be!

Points to Ponder:

A wise person once said:

1. Breaking News: Condoms don't guarantee safe sex any more. A friend of mine was wearing one when he was shot dead by the woman's husband.
2. Arguing over a woman's bust size is like choosing between Heineken, Toohey's New, XXXS Gold and VB. Men may state their preferences, but will grab whatever is available.
3. I haven't verified this on Snopes, but it sounds legit. A recent study found that women who carry a little weight live longer than the men who mention it.
4. One-fourth of the world's population lives on less than $200 a year. Ninety million people survive on less than $75 a year.
5. The words race car and kayak are the same whether they are read left to right or right to left. (A palindrome).

Life's struggles:

One day, a man walking down a path saw a butterfly cocoon that was about to open. As he watched, a small opening appeared in the cocoon. The man watched the butterfly for several hours as it struggled to force its body through that little hole. Then it seemed to stop making any progress. So the man decided to help the butterfly. He took a pair of scissors and opened the cocoon. The butterfly then emerged easily, but it had a withered body; it was tiny and its wings were shrivelled.

The man continued to watch because he expected that, at any moment, the wings would open, enlarge and expand, to be able to support the butterfly's body. Neither happened. In fact, the butterfly spent the rest of its life crawling around with a withered body and shrivelled wings. It never was able to take flight.

What the man, in his kindness and his goodwill, did not understand, was that the restricting cocoon and the struggle required for the butterfly to get through the tiny opening were nature's way of forcing liquid from the body of the butterfly into its wings, so that it would be ready for flight once it achieved its freedom from the cocoon.

Sometimes struggles are exactly what we need in our lives. If we were allowed to go through life without any obstacles, it would cripple us. We would not be as strong as we could have been. Never able to fly.

- I asked for strength – and was given difficulties to make me strong.
- I asked for wisdom – and was given problems to solve.
- I asked for prosperity – and was given a brain and brawn to work.
- I asked for courage – and was given obstacles to overcome.
- I asked for love – and was given troubled people to help.
- I asked for favours – and was given opportunities.

I received nothing I wanted, but received everything I needed. Live life without fear; confront all obstacles and know that you can overcome them.

CHAPTER 6

POLICE

Border Patrol:

Five Germans in an Audi Quattro arrive at the Italian border. The Italian Customs Officer stops them and tells them 'It'sa illegal to putta five people in a Quattro.'

'Vot do you mean it's illegal?' asks the German driver.

'Quattro meansa four,' replies the Italian official.

'Quattro is just ze name of ze fokken automobile,' the German says unbelievingly. 'Look at ze dam papers: ze car is designed to karry five persons.'

'You canta pull-a thata one on me-aa,' replies the Italian customs officer. 'Quattro meansa four. You have five-a people ina your car and thereforea youarra breaking da law.'

The German driver replies angrily, 'You idiot! Call your supervisor over. I vant to speak to someone viz more intelligence!'

'Sorry,' responds the Italian officer, 'He can'ta come. He'sa busy with-a two guys in a Fiat Uno.'

Yes, I've been drinking:

This actually happened to an Englishman in France who was totally drunk.

A French policeman stopped the Englishman's car and asked if he's been drinking.

With great difficulty, the Englishman admits that he has been drinking all day, that his daughter got married that morning, and that he drank champagne and a few bottles of wine at the reception, and many single malt scotches thereafter.

Quite upset, the policeman proceeds to alcohol-test (breath test) the Englishman and verifies that he is indeed totally sloshed.

He asks the Englishman if he knows why, under French Law, he is going to be arrested

The Englishman answers with a bit of humour, 'No sir, I do not! But while we're asking questions, do you realise that this is a British car and that my wife is driving on the other side of the car? And she hasn't touched a drop.'

Speak to the prisoner:

Bruce went to the police station and asked to speak to the burglar who had broken into his house the previous night.

'You'll get your chance in court,' the desk Sergeant Kelly told him.

'I have to know how he got into the house without waking my wife,' pleaded Bruce. 'I've been trying to do that for years.'

Two dumb robbers:

Two robbers were robbing a hotel. The first one said, 'I hear a siren. Jump.'

The second one replies, 'But we're on the 13th floor!'

The first one screams back, 'This is no time to be superstitious.'

(The first one must have been a blond.)

The recruit:

A police recruit was asked during the exam, 'What would you do if you had to arrest your own mother?'

He answered, 'Call for backup.'

Stolen car:

The proud owner of a magnificent 1956 Chevrolet convertible, wrote to say he had restored the car to perfection over the last few years, and sent this...

Last week on a very warm summer afternoon I decided to take my car to town. It needed gas, as the gauge was practically on empty, but I needed an ice cream, so I headed first to my favourite ice cream shop.

I had trouble finding a parking space and had to park it down a side street. I noticed a group of young guys standing around smoking cigarettes and eyeing my car rather covetously. I was a bit uneasy leaving it there. But people often take interest in such an old and well-preserved car, so I went off to enjoy my ice cream.

The line at the ice cream shop was long, and it took me quite a while to return to my car. When I did, my worst fears were realized... My car was gone.

I called the police and reported the theft and then went back and bought a quart of pistachio ice cream. About ten minutes later the police called me to say they had found the car abandoned near a gas station a few miles out of town.

It was unharmed and I was relieved. It seems just before I called, they had received a call from a young woman who was an employee at a self-service gas station. She told them that three young men had driven in with this beautiful old convertible. One of them came to the window and prepaid for $20 worth of gas.

Then all three of them walked around the car. Then they all got in the car and drove off, without filling the tank.

The question is, why would anybody steal a car, pay for gas that they never pumped, and then abandon the car later and walk away?

Answer: They couldn't find where to put the gas!

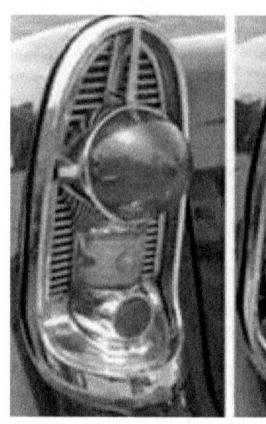 

The lane weaver:

A cop pulls a guy over for weaving across two lanes of traffic. He walks up to the driver's window and asks, 'You drinkin'?'

The driver said, 'Well that depends - You buyin'?'

Painting thief:

A thief in Paris planned to steal some paintings from the Louvre. After careful planning, he got past security, stole the paintings and made it safely to his van. However, he was captured only two blocks away when his van ran out of gas.

When asked how he could mastermind such a crime and still make such an obvious err, he replied, 'Monsieur, this is the reason I stole the paintings. I had no more money to buy Degas to make de Van Gogh.'

Thieves are getting smarter:

1. Long-term parking:

Some people left their car in the long-term parking at San Jose while away, and someone broke into the car. Using the information on the car's registration in the glove compartment, they drove the car to the people's home in Pebble Beach and robbed it. So I guess if we are going to leave the car in long-term parking, we should NOT leave the registration/insurance cards in it, nor your remote garage door opener. This gives us something to think about with all our new electronic technology.

2. GPS:

Someone had their car broken into while they were at a football game. Their car was parked on the green which was adjacent to the football stadium and specially allotted to football fans. Things stolen from the car included a garage door remote control, some money and a GPS which had been prominently mounted on the dashboard. When the victims got home, they found that their house had been ransacked and just about everything worth anything had been stolen. The thieves had used the GPS to guide them to the house. They then used the garage remote control to open the garage door and gain entry to the house. The thieves knew the owners were at the football game, they knew what time the game was scheduled to finish and so they knew how much time they had to clean out the house. It would appear that they had brought a truck to empty the house of its contents. Something to consider if you have a GPS - don't put your home address in it... Put a nearby address (like a store or gas station) so you can still find your way home if you need to, but no one else would know where you live if your GPS were stolen.

3. Mobile phones:

I never thought of this... One lady has changed her habit of how she lists her names on her cell phone after her handbag was stolen. Her handbag, which contained her cell phone, credit card, wallet, etc., was stolen. Twenty minutes later when she called her hubby, from a pay phone telling him what had happened, hubby says, 'I received your text asking about our Pin number and I've replied a little while ago.' When they rushed down to the bank, the bank staff told them all the money was already withdrawn. The thief had actually used the stolen cell phone to text 'hubby' in the contact list and got hold of the pin number. Within twenty minutes he had withdrawn all the money from their bank account.

Moral of the lesson:

a. Do not disclose the relationship between you and the people in your contact list. Avoid using names like Home, Honey, Hubby, Sweetheart, Dad, Mom, etc.
b. And very importantly, when sensitive info is being asked through texts, CONFIRM by calling back.
c. Also, when you're being texted by friends or family to meet them somewhere, be sure to call back to confirm that the message came from them. If you don't reach them, be very careful about going places to meet 'family and friends' who text you.

How to disable a stolen or missing mobile phone?

The most important thing to do is to find out the serial number of your phone BEFORE it gets stolen or goes missing Once you obtain the number, put it in a safe place for easy reference. To identify your mobile phone's serial number, pretend you are making a phone call and key in the following digits on your phone: ***#06#.**

A 15-digit code will appear on the screen. This number is unique to your mobile phone. If your phone gets stolen or you lose it, you can contact your phone service provider and give them the serial number and ask them to disable your phone. They will then be able to block your handset so even if the thief changes the SIM card - your phone will be totally useless. You probably won't get your phone back, but at least you know that whoever stole it can't use or sell it either. If everybody does this, there would be no point in people stealing mobile phones.

If it had just gone missing and you find it again, re-call your phone server and activate the phone. All of the original information will still be on the phone.

4. Purse in the grocery cart scam:

A lady went grocery-shopping at a local mall and left her purse sitting in the children's seat of the cart while she reached something off a shelf... Wait till you read the WHOLE story! Her wallet was stolen, and she reported it to the store personnel. After returning home, she received a phone call from the Mall Security to say that they had her wallet and that although there was no money in it, it did still hold her personal papers. She immediately went to pick up her wallet, only to be told by Mall Security that they had not called her. By the time she returned home again, her house had been broken into and burglarized. The thieves knew that by calling and saying they were Mall Security; they could lure her out of her house long enough for them to burglarize it.

Illegal turn:

A father in a hurry, taking his 8-year-old son to school, made a turn at a red light, where it wasn't allowed.

'Uh-oh, I just made an illegal turn!', he said.

'That's okay, Dad,' his son replied. 'The police car right behind us did the same thing.'

Quick thinking Scotsman:

A Scotsman and an Englishman were leaning against the counter in a store when a bandit walked in brandishing a gun. The Scot, a quick thinker, hauled out his money and handed it to his English friend and said, 'Here's the fifty dollars you lent me.'

The eyes have it:

A policeman pulls a man over for speeding and asks him to get out of the car. After looking the man over he says, 'Sir, I couldn't help but notice your eyes are bloodshot. Have you been drinking?'

The man gets really indignant and says, 'Officer, I couldn't help but notice your eyes are glazed. Have you been eating doughnuts?'

Vanilla Pudding Robbery:

(Excerpt from an article which appeared in The Dublin Times about a bank robbery on March 2.)

Once inside the bank shortly after midnight, their efforts at disabling the security system got underway immediately. The robbers, who expected to find one or two large safes filled with cash and valuables, were surprised to see hundreds of smaller safes throughout the bank. The robbers cracked the first safe's combination, and inside they found only a small bowl of vanilla pudding.

As recorded on the bank's audio tape system, one robber said, 'At least we'll have a bit to eat.'

The robbers opened up a second safe, and it also contained nothing but vanilla pudding. The process continued until all safes were opened. They did not find one-pound sterling, a diamond, nor an ounce of gold. Instead, all the safes contained covered little bowls of pudding. Disappointed, the robbers made a quiet exit, each leaving with nothing more than a queasy, uncomfortably full stomach.

The newspaper headline read: **'Ireland's largest sperm bank robbed early this morning'**

CHAPTER 7

TRAVEL

Relatives:

A businessman in the first class cabin decided to chat up the drop-dead, gorgeous flight attendant. 'What is your name?' he asked.

Flight attendant, 'Angela Benz, sir.'

Businessman, 'Lovely name – any relation to Mercedes Benz?'

Flight attendant, 'Yes sir, very close.'

Businessman, 'How close?'

Flight attendant, 'Same price.'

The graveyard:

A tourist in Vienna was going through a graveyard when he heard music. No one was around, so he starts searching for the source. He finally locates the origin and finds it's coming from a grave with a headstone that read: 'Ludwig van Beethoven, 1770 – 1827. Then he realizes that the music is Beethoven's Ninth Symphony and it's being played backward!

Puzzled, he leaves the graveyard and persuades a friend to return with him. By the time they arrive back at the grave, the music has changed. This time it's the Seventh Symphony, but like the previous piece, it's being played backwards.

Curious, the men agree to consult a music scholar. When they return with the expert, the Fifth Symphony is playing – again backwards. The expert notices that the symphonies are being played in the reverse order in which they were composed. By the next day, the word was spread, and a crowd gathered at the gravesite. They were all listening to the Second Symphony being played backward.

Just then the graveyard's caretaker ambles up to the group. Someone in the group asks him if he has an explanation for the music. 'I would have thought it was obvious,' the caretaker said, 'he's decomposing.'

Female pilot:

When I was in the pub, I heard a couple of blokes saying that they wouldn't feel safe on an aircraft if they knew the pilot was a woman. What a pair of sexists. I mean, it's not as if she'd have to reverse the bloody thing!

What happened?

As the pilot climbs out of a plane having crashed, tearing off the wings and tail; a crash truck arrives.

A rescuer asks the bloodied pilot, 'What happened?'

The pilot replies, 'I don't know – I just got here myself.'

The new-born:

Bring a new-born on a plane, and you get 'The Look.' Not one of 'Oh, what a cute baby.' It's more 'Please, God, don't let that mum sit next to me.' So when our baby began to wail just after take-off, you could have cut the tension with a Tickle Me Elmo doll. Was my wife rattled? Not at all. She lullabied our daughter with, 'I'm teething, on a jet plane. Don't know when I'll be calm again.'

Taking care of luggage:

A young man was heading home to spend the holidays with his parents. When he got to the airline counter, he presented his ticket to Brisbane. He then gave the agent his luggage and said, 'I'd like you to send my red suitcase to Bermuda and my green suitcase to London.'

'I'm sorry sir, but we can't do that,' replied the confused agent.

'Really?' replied the young man. 'Well, I'm very relieved to hear you say that, because that's exactly what you did to my luggage last year.'

George and the dragon:

A poor vagabond, travelling a country road in England, tired and hungry, came to a roadside inn with a sign reading, 'George and the Dragon.'

He knocked, the innkeeper's wife stuck her head out a window.

'Could ye spare some food?' he asked.

The woman glanced at his shabby clothes and obviously poor condition.

'No!' she said rather sternly.

'Could I have a pint of ale?'

'No,' she snapped again.

'Could I at least sleep in your stable?"

'No!'

By this time, she was fairly shouting. The vagabond tried again, 'Might I please…?'

'What now?' the woman interrupted impatiently.

'D'ye suppose I might have a word with George?'

Two blind pilots:

Two blind pilots were both wearing dark glasses. One is using a guide dog and the other is tapping his way along the aisle with a cane.

Nervous laughter spreads through the cabin, but the men enter the cockpit, the door closes and the engines start up. The passengers begin glancing nervously around, searching for some sign that this is just a little practical joke. None is forthcoming.

The plane moves faster and faster down the runway and the people sitting in the window seats realize they're headed straight for the water at the edge of the airport. As it begins to look as though the plane will plough into the water, panicked screams fill the cabin.

At that moment, the plane lifts smoothly into the air. The passengers relax and laugh a little sheepishly and soon all retreat into their magazines, secure in the knowledge that the plane is in good hands

In the cockpit, one of the blind pilots turns to the other and says, 'Ya know, Bob, one of these days, they're gonna scream too late and we're all gonna die.'

Four parachutes:

An airplane was about to crash; there were five passengers on board, but only four parachutes.

The first passenger, Holly Madison said, 'I have my own reality show and I'm the smartest and prettiest woman at playboy, so Americans don't want me to die.' she took the first pack and jumped out of the plane.

The second passenger, John McCain, said, 'I'm a senator, and a decorated war hero from an elite navy unit from the United States of America.' So he grabbed the second pack and jumped.

The third passenger, Donald Trump said, 'I'm going to be the next president of the United States, I'm the smartest man in our country, and I will make America great again.' so he grabbed the pack next to him and jumped out.

The fourth passenger, Billy Graham, said to the fifth passenger, a 10-year-old schoolgirl, 'I have lived a full life and served my God the best I could. I will sacrifice my life and let you have the last parachute.'

The little girl said, 'That's okay, Mr. Graham. There's a parachute left for you. The smartest man in America took my school bag.'

Unusual international signs:

- In a Bangkok Temple: It is forbidden to enter a woman, even a foreigner, if dressed as a man.
- Cocktail Lounge, Norway: Ladies are requested not to have children in the bar.
- Doctor's Office, Rome: Specialist in women and other diseases.
- Dry Cleaners, Bangkok: Drop your trousers here for the best results.
- A Nairobi Restaurant: Customers, who find our waitresses rude, ought to see the manager.
- On the main road to Mombasa, leaving Nairobi: Take notice: when this sign is under water, this road is impassable.
- On a poster at Kencom: Are you an adult that cannot read? If so, we can help.
- In a City restaurant: Open seven days a week and weekends.
- In a Cemetery: Persons are prohibited from picking flowers, from any but their own graves.
- Tokyo hotel's rules and regulations: Guests are requested not to smoke, or do other disgusting behaviours, in bed.
- On the menu of a Swiss Restaurant: Our wines leave you nothing to hope for.
- In a Tokyo Bar: Special cocktails for the ladies with nuts.
- Hotel, Yugoslavia: The flattening of underwear with pleasure is the job of the chambermaid.
- Hotel, Japan: You are invited to take advantage of the chambermaid.
- In the lobby of a Moscow Hotel, across from a Russian Orthodox Monastery: You are welcome to visit the cemetery, where famous Russian and Soviet composers, artists, and writers are buried daily, except Thursday.

- A sign posted in Germany's Black Forest: It is strictly forbidden on our black forest camping site, that people of different sex, for instance, men and women, live together in one tent, unless they are married with each other for this purpose.
- Hotel, Zurich: Because of the impropriety of entertaining guests of the opposite sex in the bedroom, it is suggested that the lobby be used for this purpose.
- Advertisement for donkey rides, Thailand: Would you like to ride on your own ass?
- Airline ticket office, Copenhagen: We take your bags and send them in all directions.
- A Laundry in Rome: Ladies, leave your clothes here and then spend the afternoon having a good time.
- And finally, the all-time classic, seen in an Abu Dhabi Souk shop window: If the front is closed, please enter through my backside.

Breaking the rules"

A man and a woman are seated next to each other on a flight. They start eyeing each other, have a discussion and bot realise that they want to do the same thing. He slips a condom out of his pocket, and she looks delighted.

'Rear toilet?' he suggests.

'Five minutes', she agrees and goes off. He waits five minutes, then goes and slips in there with her.

'Right, get that condom on,' she says.

Soon they are both signing with pleasure, but the sharp eyed-stewardess has noticed them and realised what they were up to. So she humiliates them by making an announcement over the PA system.

'To the lady and gentleman in the rear toilet, we know what you're doing and it is expressly forbidden by airline regulations. Now please put those cigarettes out and take the condom off the smoke detector.'

[I just threw that one in for you dirty minded people.]

Where are we?

Nights in England are coal black, making parachute jumps difficult and dangerous. So we attach small lights called chemlites to our jumpsuits to make ourselves visible to the rest of our team.

Late one night, lost after a practice jump, we knocked on the door of a small cottage. When a woman answered, she was greeted by the sight of five men festooned in glowing chemlites. 'Excuse me,' I said. 'Can you tell me where we are?'

In a thick English accent, the woman replied, 'Earth.'

Trip to Beijing:

A friend went to Beijing recently and was given this brochure by the hotel. It is precious. She is keeping it and reading it whenever she feels depressed. Obviously, it has been translated directly, word for word from Mandarin to English.

Getting There:

Our representative will make you wait at the airport. The bus to the hotel runs along the lake shore. Soon you will feel pleasure in passing water. You will know that you are getting near the hotel, because you will go round the bend. The manager will await you in the entrance hall. He always tries to have intercourse with all new guests.

The Hotel:

This is a family hotel, so children are very welcome. We of course are always pleased to accept adultery. Highly skilled nurses are available in the evenings to put down your children. Guests are invited to conjugate in the bar and expose themselves to others. But please note that ladies are not allowed to have babies in the bar. We organize social games, so no guest is ever left alone to play with them self.

The Restaurant:

Our menus have been carefully chosen to be ordinary and unexciting. At dinner, our quartet will circulate from table to table, and fiddle with you.

Your Room:

Every room has excellent facilities for your private parts. In winter, every room is on heat. Each room has a balcony offering views of outstanding obscenity! You will not be disturbed by traffic noise, since the road between the hotel and the lake is used only by pederasts.

Bed:

Your bed has been made in accordance with local tradition. If you have any other ideas, please ring for the chambermaid. Please take advantage of her. She will be very pleased to squash your shirts, blouses and underwear. If asked, she will also squeeze your trousers.

Above All:

When you leave us at the end of your holiday, you will have no hope. You will struggle to forget it.

CHAPTER 8

CHILDREN

Father and son:

A father and his nine-year-old son had spent a Saturday morning fishing and had laughed and enjoyed their morning. They were at a McDonalds enjoying a hamburger when the boy asked his father whether he could tell him a joke. The father nodded and said, 'Sure,' but wondered what kind of joke he would tell him.

The boy asked, 'I need a piece of paper and a pen to tell this joke.'

His father pulled out a pen and gave him a napkin, 'Will this do?'

'Sure,' the boy replied and wrote two words on the napkin.

'You have to say these two words out loud,' he explained as he handed the napkin to his father.

His father complied, frowned, then laughed out loud. 'You got me with that one!' he exclaimed as he gave his son a high five.

The two words were 'hoof hearted.' Say it out loud and you will likely laugh yourself.

Taxi ride:

A woman and her twelve-year-old son were riding through a notorious part of town. It was raining and all the prostitutes were standing under awnings.

'Mom,' asked the boy, 'what are all those women doing?'

'They're waiting for their husbands to get off work,' she replied.

The taxi driver turned around and said, 'Geez lady! Why don't you tell him the truth? They're hookers, boy! They have sex with men for money.'

The boy's eyes get wide and he says, 'Is that true Mom?'

His mother, glaring hard at the driver, finally answers 'Yes.'

After a few minutes, the kid asks, 'Mom, if those women have babies, what happens to them?'

Still glaring at the driver she replied, 'Most of them become taxi drivers.'

Food:

Teacher, 'Kids, what does the chicken give you?'

Student, 'Meat.'

Teacher, 'Very good. Now what does the pig give you?'

Student, 'Bacon.'

Teacher, 'Great. And what does the fat cow give you?'

Student, 'Homework.'

Family planning lesson:

Six-year-old Annie returned home from school and explained to her mother that her class had had its first family planning lesion.

Her mother, very interested, asked, 'Oh... How did it go?'

'I nearly died of shame!'; the girl answered. 'Sam from down the street says the stork brings babies. Sally next door said you can buy babies at the orphanage. And Pete says you can buy babies at the hospital.'

Her mother answers laughingly, 'But that's no reason to be ashamed.'

'No... but I can't tell them that we were so poor that you had to do it yourselves.'

The school play:

A boy comes home from school and excitedly tells his dad that he had obtained a part in the school play. He was playing a man who had been married for twenty-five years.

The dad replied, 'Never mind son, maybe next year you'll get a speaking part.'

Spring fever:

Four high school boys, affected with spring fever, skipped morning classes. After lunch they reported to the teacher that they had a flat tire. Much to their relief, she smiled, then said, 'Well, you missed a test today, so take your seats apart from each other and take out a piece of paper.'

Still smiling, she waited for them to sit down, then said, 'First question: Which tire was flat?'

Big woman:

I was standing in a queue behind a very fat woman with a huge arse when her phone started to beep. My young son backed up and shouted, 'Watch out – she's reversing!'

At the library:

A little boy walked up to the librarian to check out a book entitled 'Comprehensive guide for mothers.'

When the librarian asked him if it was for his mother, he answered 'no.'

'Then why are you checking it out?'

'Because,' said the little boy confidently, 'I just started collecting moths last month!'

Little Johnny:

1. Little Johnny was in the classroom bored to the back teeth on a Friday afternoon, and the teacher decided to have a game for the kids to get them thinking.

'Okay class. Now I'm going to say a famous quote, and the first person to tell me who said that quote, can have Monday off.' said the teacher.

'Who is credited with writing the phrase, 'To be or not to be, that is the question?'' asked the teacher.

Little Pham Lam Nguyen at the front of the class called out, 'Shakespeare'

'Well done!' said the teacher, 'You can have Monday off.'

'No thank you Miss. I am of Vietnamese origin and it is in our culture to study as hard as we can, so I will be here on Monday studying hard.' said Little Pham Lam Nguyen.

'Well okay,' said the teacher. The next quote is, 'I had a dream!'

Little Fri Sum Kat also at the front yelled out 'I bereiva it was Martin Ruther King!'

'Well done!' said the teacher. 'You can have Monday off.'

'No thanka you miss I am of Chinese oligin and we also do not take time offa school. Education is evelything to us, so I will be in on Monday studying hard too.' said little Fri Sum Kat.

'Okay,' said the teacher.

Then she heard a voice from the back of the classroom, 'Damned Asians!'

'Who said that?' yelled the teacher in an angry tone.

'Donald Trump!' yelled little Johnny. 'See ya on Tuesday.'

2. Little Johnny walked into class every morning with a black eye. After a while his teacher got worried and asked him about it.

Johnny's answer was: 'Our house is very small, miss. Me, my mother and my father, we sleep on the same bed. Every night my father asks, 'Johnny are you sleeping?' Then I say 'No' and then he slaps my face and gives me a black eye.'

So the teacher says to him, 'Tonight when your father asks again, keep dead quiet and don't answer'.

The following morning Little Johnny comes to school and his eye is fine, so the teacher breathes a sigh of relief, but the day after that Johnny comes back with a severe black eye again.

'My goodness Johnny, why the black eye again?'

He tells her: 'Miss, Dad asked me again, 'Johnny are you sleeping?... and I shut up and kept dead still. Then my father and my mother started moving, you know at the same time, Mum was breathing erratically, kicking her legs up frantically and squealing like a demented hyena on the bed'... Then my father asks my mother: 'Are you coming?' Then my mum says, 'Yes I'm coming, are you coming too?' and my dad answered 'Yes'.

They don't usually go anywhere without me, so I said 'Wait for me!'

3. Little Johnnie's neighbour had a baby. Unfortunately, the baby was born without ears.

   When mother and new baby came home from the hospital, Johnnie's family was invited over to see the baby. Before they left their house, Little Johnnie's dad had a talk with him and explained that the baby had no ears. His dad also told him that if he so much mentioned anything about the baby's missing ears or even said the word ears, he would get the smacking of his life when they came back home.

   Little Johnnie told his dad he understood completely.

When Johnnie looked in the crib he said, 'What a beautiful baby.'

The mother said, 'Why, thank you, Little Johnnie.

Johnnie said, 'He has beautiful little feet and beautiful little hands, a cute little nose and really beautiful eyes. Can he see?'

'Yes', the mother replied, 'we are so thankful; the Doctor said he will have 20/20 vision.'

'That's great', said Little Johnnie,' kuz he'd be in big trouble if he needed glasses'.

4. The nun teaching Sunday School was speaking to her class one morning and she asked the question, 'When you die and go to Heaven, which part of your body goes first?

Suzy raised her hand and said, 'I think it's your hands.'

'Why do you think it's your hands, Suzy?'

Suzy replied, 'Because when you pray, you hold your hands together in front of you and God just takes your hands first.

'What a wonderful answer!' the nun said.

Little Johnny raised his hand and said, 'Sister, I think it's your feet.

The nun looked at him with the strangest look on her face. 'Now Johnny, why do you think it would be your feet?'

Little Johnny said, 'Well, I walked into Mommy and Daddy's bedroom the other night. Mommy had her legs straight up in the air and she was saying, 'Oh God, I'm coming.' I gotta tell you, if Dad hadn't pinned her down, we'd have lost her.'

The Nun fainted.

5. It was breakfast time and Dad and Johnny were munching away on their cereal. Mom comes down the stairs and says, 'I'm not pregnant.'

   Dad, still reading the paper mutters, 'That's good news.'

   Jonny goes off to school and in class is asked, 'What's your good news today, Johnny?

   'I'm not pregnant, Miss,' is his answer.

6. Eight-year-old little Johnny asked his mother the age-old question: 'How did I get here?

   His mother told him, 'God sent you.'

   'And my Cousin Matt?'

   'He sent him also,' said the mother.

   'Did God send you, too?' asked little Johnny.

   'Yes, dear,' the mother replied.

   'Did God send dad, too?' asked little Johnny.

   'Yes, dear,' the mother replied.

   'What about Grandma and Grandpa?' Johnny persisted.

   'He sent them also,' the mother said.

   'Did He send their parents, too?' little Johnny asked.

   'Yes, dear, He did,' said the mother patiently.

   'So you're telling me that there has been no sex in this family for 200 years? No wonder everyone's so grumpy around here.'

7. Sunday School teacher of preschoolers was concerned that his students might be a little confused about Jesus Christ because of the Christmas season emphasis on His birth. He wanted to make sure they understood that the birth of Jesus occurred a long time ago, that He grew up, etc.

   So he asked his class, 'Where is Jesus today?'

Steven raised his hand and said, 'He's in heaven.'

Mary was called on and answered, 'He's in my heart.'

Little Johnny, waving his hand furiously, blurted out, 'I know! I know! He's in our bathroom!!!'

The whole class got very quiet, looked at the teacher, and waited for a response. The teacher was completely at a loss for a few very long seconds. He finally gathered his wits and asked Little Johnny how he knew this.

And Little Johnny said, 'Well...every morning, my father gets up, bangs on the bathroom door, and yells... 'Jesus Christ... are you still in there?'

8. A hopeful politician was visiting a primary school and the class was in the middle of a discussion related to words and their meanings. The teacher asked the politician if he would like to lead the discussion on the word 'tragedy.'

He did so and a little boy stood up and offered, 'If my best friend who lives on a farm, is playing in a field and a tractor runs over him and kills him – that would be a tragedy.'

'Incorrect,' said the politician, 'that would be an accident.'

A little girl raised her hand, 'If a school bus was carrying fifty children drove over a cliff, killing everybody inside – that would be a tragedy.'

'I'm afraid not,' explained the politician, 'that's what we would refer to as a great loss.'

The room went silent. No other children volunteered until Little Johnny raised his hand and said, 'If a plane carrying several top politicians was struck by a friendly fire missile and blown to smithereens, that would be a tragedy.'

'Fantastic,' exclaimed the politician, 'and can you tell me why that would be a tragedy?'

'Well, said Johnny, 'It has to be a tragedy, because it certainly wouldn't be a great loss, and it probably wouldn't be an accident either!'

9. Hillary Clinton went to a gifted-student primary school in New York to talk about the world. After her talk she offers question time. One little boy put up his hand. Hillary asks him what his name is.

'Kenneth," he replies

'And what is your question, Kenneth?' she asks.

'I have three questions,' he says.

'First - whatever happened in Benghazi? Second why would you run for president if you are not capable of handling two e-mail accounts? And, third - whatever happened to the missing six billion dollars while you were secretary of state?'

Just then the bell rings for recess. Hillary informs the kiddies that they will continue after recess.

When they resume Hillary says, 'Okay, where were we? Oh, that's right, question time. Who has a question?'

A different boy, little Johnny - puts his hand up. Hillary points to him and asks him what his name is.

'Johnny,' he says.

'And what is your question, Johnny?' she asks.

'I have five questions," he says. 'First - whatever happened in Benghazi? Second - why would you run for president if you are not capable of handling two e-mail accounts? Third - whatever happened to the missing six billion dollars while you were secretary of state? Fourth - why did the recess bell go off twenty minutes early? And, fifth - where the hell is Kenneth?'

Personal questions:

A mother is driving her little girl to her friend's house for a play date.

'Mommy,' the little girl asks, 'how old are you?'

'Honey, you are not supposed to ask a lady her age,' the mother replied. 'It's not polite.'

'Okay,' the little girl says, 'what colour was your hair two years ago?'

'Now really,' the mother says, 'those are personal questions and are really none of your business.'

Undaunted, the little girl asks, 'Why did you and Daddy get a divorce?'

'That's enough questions, young lady! Honestly!'

The exasperated mother walks away as the two friends begin to play.

'My Mom won't tell me anything about her,' the little girl says to her friend.

'Well,' says the friend, 'all you need to do is look at her driver's license. It's like a report card, it has everything on it.'

Later that night the little girl says to her mother, 'I know how old you are. You are 32.'

The mother is surprised and asks, 'How did you find that out?'

'I also know that you used to have brown hair.'

The mother is past surprised and shocked now. 'How in Heaven's name did you find that out?'

'And,' the little girl says triumphantly, 'I know why you and daddy got a divorce.'

'Oh really?' the mother asks. 'Why?'

'Because on your driving license it says you got an 'F' in sex.'

Where babies come from:

On the way back from a Cub meeting, my grandson innocently said to my son, 'Dad, I know babies come from mommies' tummies, but how do they get there in the first place?'

After my son hemmed and hawed awhile, my grandson finally spoke up in disgust, 'You don't have to make up something, Dad. It's okay if you don't know the answer.'

Toy raffle:

A father of five small kids won a toy in a raffle at his work. That night when he got home, he called the kids together to ask them which one should get the prize.

'Who is the most obedient?' he asked, 'Who never talks back to their Mom? Who does everything Mom says?'

Finally, the eldest puts up his hand and says, 'Okay Dad, you get the toy!'

The handyman:

The proud father brought home a backyard swing set for his children and immediately started to assemble it with all the neighbourhood children anxiously waiting to play on it.

After several hours of reading the directions, attempting to fit bolt A into slot B, etc., he finally gave up and called upon an old handyman working in a neighbouring yard.

The old-timer came over, threw the directions away, and in a short while had the set completely assembled.

'It's beyond me,' said the father, 'how you got it together without even reading instructions.'

'To tell the truth,' replied the old-timer, 'I can't read, and when you can't read, you've got to think.'

What do you want out of life?

A teacher asked her class, 'What do you want out of life?'

A little girl in the back row raised her hand and said, 'All I want out of life is four little animals, just like my Mom always says.'

The teacher asked, 'Really and what four little animals would that be?'

The little girl said, 'A mink on my back, a jaguar in the garage, a tiger in the bed and a jackass to pay for all of it.

The teacher got a coughing fit and had to leave the room.

Problem child:

The mother of a problem child was advised by a psychiatrist, 'You are far too upset and worried about your son. I suggest you take tranquilizers regularly.'

On her next visit the psychiatrist asked, 'Have the tranquilizers calmed you down?'

'Yes,' the boy's mother answered.

'And how is your son now?' the psychiatrist asked.

'Who cares?' the mother replied.

Three simple rules in life:

1. If you do not GO after what you want – you'll never have it.
2. If you do not ASK, the answer will always be No.
3. If you do not STEP forward, you'll always be in the same place.

CHAPTER 9

SENIORS

Growing old is hard work... The mind says 'yes' but the body says, 'What the hell are you thinking.'

Alzheimer's Disease:

I told you that I don't have Alzheimer's disease. I have 'Sometimer's disease,' sometimes I remember and sometimes I don't.

The lions:

Two old men are drinking in a bar. One says, 'Did you know that Lions have sex ten to fifteen times a day?'

'Oh bugger!' says his friend, 'and I just joined Rotary!'

The new alphabet:

A is for apple, and B is for boat - that used to be right, but now it won't float! Age before beauty is what we once said, but let's be a bit more realistic instead. Here's the new alphabet:

A's for arthritis; B's the bad back, C's the chest pains, perhaps car-di-ac? D is for dental decay and decline, E is for eyesight, can't read that top line! F is for farting and fluid retention, G is for gut droop, which I'd rather not mention.

H high blood pressure - I'd rather it low; I for incisions with scars you can show. J is for joints, out of socket, won't mend, K is for knees that crack when they bend. L is for libido, what happened to sex? M is for memory - I forget what comes next. N is neuralgia, in nerves way down low; O is for osteo, bones that don't grow!

P for prescriptions, I have quite a few, just give me a pill and I'll be good as new! Q is for queasy, is it fatal or flu? R is for reflux; one meal turns to two.

S is for sleepless nights, counting my fears, T is for Tinnitus; bells in my ears! U is for urinary; troubles with flow; V for vertigo, that's 'dizzy,' you know.

W for worry, now what's going 'round? X is for X ray, and what might be found. Y for another year I'm left here behind, Z is for zest I still have - in my mind!

I've survived all the symptoms, my body's deployed, and I'm keeping twenty-six doctors fully employed!

P.S.: If you can't afford a doctor – go to the airport – you'll get a free x-ray and a breast exam and: if you mention Al Qaeda, you'll get a free colonoscopy.

The New wife:

Mr. Peabody, the local banker, saw his old friend Tom, an 80-year-old rancher, in town. Tom had lost his wife the year before. Rumour had it he was marrying a 'mail order' bride.

Mr. Peabody asked Tom if the rumour was true.

Tom replied, 'Yes, it is true.'

Mr. Peabody asked, 'May I ask the age of your new bride to be?'

Tom replied, 'She'll be 21 in November.'

Mr. Peabody, being a wise man, knew the sexual appetite of a young woman could not be satisfied by an 80-year-old man. Mr. Peabody wanted Tom's remaining years to be happy. So he tactfully suggested that Tom should consider getting a hired hand to help him out on the ranch, knowing nature would take its own course.

Tom thought this was a good idea and said he would look for a hired hand that very afternoon.

Four months later, Mr. Peabody saw Tom in town again.

Mr. Peabody asked, 'How is your new wife?'

Tom replied, 'Good. She's pregnant.'

Mr. Peabody was pleased his sage advice had worked out so well. He asked, 'And how's the hired hand?'

Without hesitating, Tom said, 'She's pregnant too!'

Never underestimate old men.

Depends:

Just because something is fashionable or tempting does not make it correct. Someone has finally explained the reason baby nappies have brand names such as 'Luvs' and 'Huggies,' while undergarments for old people are called 'Depends.' You see, when babies poop their pants, people are still gonna Luv 'em and Hug 'em. However, when old people poop their pants, it 'Depends' on who's in the Will.

Terrorism:

The degree of terrorism these days is causing me problems. When I was at the checkout and ready to pay for my groceries the cashier said, 'Strip down, facing me.'

Making a mental note so I could complain to my local MP about this security rubbish, I did just as she had instructed.

After the shrieking and hysterical remarks of those nearby finally subsided, I found out that she was referring to how I should position my bank card.

Nonetheless, I've been asked to shop elsewhere in the future. The need to make their instructions a little clearer for seniors. I hate this getting older stuff.

Having Sex:

Men between 60 and 80 years of age will on average, have sex two to three times per week (and a small number a lot more – whereas "Chinese men, in exactly the same age group, will have sex only once or twice per year if they're lucky).

This has come as very upsetting news to both me and most of my mates, as none of us had any idea we were Chinese.

Definition of old:

I very quietly confided to my best friend that I was having an affair. She turned to me and asked, 'Are you having it catered?'

And that, my friend, is the sad definition of 'Old.'

Parkinson's or Alzheimer's:

An older woman was asked, 'At your ripe age, what would you prefer to get - Parkinson's or Alzheimer's?'

The wise one answered, 'Definitely Parkinson's! It's better to spill half my wine than to forget where I keep the bottle!'

The importance of having an occupation after retirement:

As we get older we sometimes begin to doubt our ability to 'make a difference' in the world. It's at these times that our hopes are boosted by the remarkable achievements of other 'seniors' who have found the courage to take on challenges that would make many of us wither.

Harold Schlumberg is such a person who says: 'I've often been asked, 'What do you do now that you're retired?' Well, I'm fortunate to have a chemical engineering background and one of the things I enjoy most is converting beer, wine and whiskey into urine. It's rewarding, uplifting, satisfying and fulfilling. 'I do it every day and I really enjoy it.'

Harold is an inspiration to us all.

The golden years:

Several days ago as I left a meeting, I desperately gave myself a personal search as I was looking for my car keys. They were not in my pockets. A quick search in the meeting room revealed nothing.

I suddenly realised that I must have left them in the car. Frantically, I headed for the car park. My husband had scolded me many times for leaving the keys in the ignition.

My theory is that the ignition is the best place NOT to lose them. His theory is that the car will be stolen.

As I scanned the car park, I came to the horrifying conclusion! His theory was right. The car park was empty.

I immediately called the police, gave them my location and confessed that I must have left my keys in the car and that it had been stolen. I then made the most difficult call of all – I phoned my husband.

'Hello my love,' I stammered. I always called him 'My love' at times like these. 'I left my keys in the car and it's been stolen.'

There was a period of silence. I thought the call had disconnected, but then I heard his voice as he barked, 'Don't you remember. I dropped you off!'

Now it was my time to be silent. Embarrassed, I said, 'Well, come and get me.'

He retorted, 'I will as soon as I convince this policeman that I have not stolen your car.

This is what they call, 'The golden years!'

Sportsmanship:

At one point during a game, the coach said to one of his young players, 'Do you understand what cooperation is? What a team is?'

The little boy nodded in the affirmative.

'Do you understand that what matters is whether we win together as a team?'

The little boy nodded yes.

'So,' the coach continued, 'when a red card is shown, you're out, you don't argue or curse or attack the umpire. Do you understand all that?'

Again the little boy nodded.

'Good,' said the coach. 'Now go over there and explain it to your grandmother.'

Seniors' complex:

On the first day at the new seniors' complex, the manager addressed all the new seniors, pointing out some of the rules. 'The female sleeping quarters will be out-of-bounds for all males, and the male dormitory to the females. Anyone caught breaking this rule will be fined $20 the first time.' He continued, 'Anyone caught breaking this rule the second time will be fined $60, being caught a third time will cost you a fine of $180. Are there any questions?'

At this point, an older gentleman stood up in the crowd and inquired, 'How much for a season pass?'

A.A.A.D.D.:

Recently, I was diagnosed with A. A. A. D. D. – Age Activated Attention Deficit Disorder. This is how it manifests itself:

- I decide to water my garden.
- As I turn on the hose in the driveway, I look over at my car and decide my car needs washing.
- As I start toward the garage, I notice that there is mail on the porch table that I brought up from the mail box earlier.
- I decide to go through the mail before I wash the car.
- I lay my car keys down on the table, put the junk mail in the rubbish bin under the table, and notice that the bin is full.
- So, I decide to put the bills back on the table and take out the rubbish first.
- But then I think, since I'm going to be near the mailbox when I take out the garbage anyway, I may as well pay the bills first.
- I take my cheque book off the table, and see that there is only one cheque left. My extra cheques are in my desk

in the study, so I go inside the house to my desk where I find the can of coke that I had been drinking.
- I'm going to look for my cheques, but first I need to push the coke aside so that I don't accidentally knock it over. I see that the coke is getting warm, and I decide I should put it in the refrigerator to keep it cold.
- As I head toward the kitchen with the coke, a vase of flowers on the counter catches my eye: they need to be watered.
- I place the coke down on the work surface, and I discover my reading glasses that I've been searching for all morning.
- I decide I better put them back on my desk, but first I'm going to water the flowers.
- I set the glasses back down on the work top, fill a container with water and suddenly I spot the TV remote. Someone has left it on the kitchen table.
- I realise that tonight when we go to watch TV, I will be looking for the remote, but I won't remember that it's on the kitchen table, so I decide to put it back in the lounge where it belongs, but first I'll water the flowers.
- I pour some water in the flowers, but quite a bit of it spills on the floor. So, I set the remote back down on the table, get some towels and wipe up the spill.
- Then, I head down the hall trying to remember what I was planning to do.

Sound familiar

Rye bread:

Two old guys, one 80 and one 87, were sitting on their usual park bench one morning. The 87-year-old had just finished his morning jog and wasn't even short of breath. The 80-year-old was amazed at his friend's stamina and asked him what he did to have so much energy.

The 87-year-old said, 'Well, I eat rye bread every day. It keeps your energy level high and you'll have great stamina with the ladies.'

So on the way home the 80-year-old stops at the bakery. As he was looking around, the lady asked if he needed any help. He said, 'Do you have any rye bread?'

She replied, 'Yes, there's a whole shelf of it. Would you like some?'

He said, 'I want five loaves.'

She said, 'My goodness, five loaves! By the time you get to the third loaf, it'll be hard.'

He replied, 'I can't believe it. Everybody knows about this but me.'

The old geezer:

An old geezer became very bored in retirement and decided to open a medical clinic.

He put a sign up outside that said: 'Dr. Geezer's clinic. Get your treatment for $500, if not cured, get back $1,000.'

Doctor 'Young,' who was positive that this old geezer didn't know beans about medicine, thought this would be a great opportunity to get $1,000, so he went to Dr. Geezer's clinic.

Dr. Young: 'Dr. Geezer, I've lost all taste in my mouth. Can you please help me??'

Dr. Geezer: 'Nurse, please bring medicine from box 22 and put 3 drops in Dr. Young's mouth.'

Dr. Young: 'Aaagh! This is Gasoline!'

Dr. Geezer: 'Congratulations! You've got your taste back. That will be $500.'

Dr. Young gets annoyed and goes back after a couple of days figuring to recover his money.

Dr. Young: 'I have lost my memory; I cannot remember anything.'

Dr. Geezer: 'Nurse, please bring medicine from box 22 and put 3 drops in the patient's mouth.'

Dr. Young: 'Oh, no you don't – that's gasoline!"

Dr. Geezer: 'Congratulations! You've got your memory back. That will be $500.'

Dr. Young (after having lost $1000) leaves angrily and comes back after several more days.

Dr. Young: 'My eyesight has become weak - I can hardly see anything!'

Dr. Geezer: 'Well, I don't have any medicine for that so, here's your $1000 back' (giving him a $10 bill.)

Dr. Young: 'But this is only $10!'

Dr. Geezer: 'Congratulations! You've got your vision back! That will be $500.

Moral of story - Just because you're young doesn't mean that you can outsmart an 'old Geezer.'

Remember: Don't make old people mad. We don't like being old in the first place, so it doesn't take much to tick us off.

A retired person's perspective:

1. I'm not saying let's go kill all the stupid people. I'm just saying let's remove all the warning labels and let the problem work itself out.
2. I changed my car horn to gunshot sounds. People move out of the way much faster now.
3. You can tell a lot about a woman's mood just be looking at her hands. If they're holding a gun, she's probably very cross.
4. Gone are the days when girls cooked like their mothers. Now they drink like their fathers.

5. You know that tingly little feeling you get when you really like someone you've just met. That's common sense leaving your body.
6. I don't like making plans for the day because then the word 'premeditated' gets thrown around in the courtroom.
7. I didn't make it to the gym today. That makes 1,508 days in a row.
8. I decided to change calling the bathroom 'the John' and renamed it 'the Jim.' I feel so much better saying 'I went to the Jim this morning.'
9. Dear paranoid people, who check behind shower curtains for murderers. If you found one, what would be your plan?
10. Teach your granddaughter how to shoot, because a restraining order is just a piece of paper.
11. I just spent fifteen minutes searching for my phone in my car, using my phone as a torch.
12. There is always a lot to be thankful for, if you take the time to look. For example, I'm sitting here thinking how nice it is that wrinkles don't hurt.
13. The best way to get rid of kitchen odours – eat out!
14. I don't understand how I can remember every word of a song from 1964, but I can't remember why I walked into the kitchen?
15. When I get old, I'm going to keep clicking my Life Alert button to see how many hot firefighters show up.
16. Here are the seven dwarfs of old age: Nappy, Wrinkly, Squinty, Rocky, Saggy, Farty and Leaky.
17. The sad part about getting old is that you stay younger on the inside but nobody can tell any more.
18. Don't be afraid of growing older. You'll still do stupid things – only slower.

When you're over 70:

1. I was standing at the bar one night, minding my own business. This fat ugly chick came up behind me,

grabbed my behind and said, 'You're kind'a cute. You got a phone number?'
I said, 'Yeah, you got a pen?'
She said, 'Yeah, I got a pen.'
I said, 'You'd better get back in it before the farmer misses you.'
Cost me 6 stitches, but when you're over seventy – who cares?

2. I was telling a woman in the pub about my ability to guess what day a woman was born just by feeling her breasts.
'Really?' she said, 'Go on then... Try.'
After about thirty seconds of fondling, she began to lose patience and said, 'Come on, what day was I born?'
'Yesterday' I replied.
Cost me a kick in the nuts, but when you're over seventy, who cares?

3. I got caught taking a pee in the swimming pool today. The lifeguard shouted at me so loud, I nearly fell in.
Cost me a bloody nose, but when you're over seventy, who cares?

4. I went to the pub last night and saw a big woman dancing on the table.
I said, 'Good legs.'
The woman giggled and said, 'Do you really think so.'
I replied, 'Definitely! Most tables would have collapsed by now.'
Cost me 6 more stitches, but when you're over seventy, who cares.

5. She: I think you need a hearing test.
He: Why the heck do I need a hairy chest?

A little philosophy:

Two 90-year-old men, Phil and Joe, had been friends all of their lives. When it was clear that Phil was dying, Joe visited him every day.

One day, Joe said, 'Phil, we both loved playing baseball all our lives, and we played all through high school. Please do me one favour: when you get to heaven, somehow you must let me know if there's baseball there.'

Phil looked up at Joe from his deathbed and said, 'Joe, you've been my best friend for many years. If it's at all possible, I'll do this favour for you.'

Shortly after that, Phil died.

A few nights later, Joe was awakened from a sound sleep by a blinding flash of white light and a voice calling out to him, 'Joe, Joe.'

'Who is it,' asked Joe, sitting up suddenly. 'Who is it?'

'Joe - it's me, Phil.'

'You're not Phil. Phil just died.'

'I'm telling you, it's me, Phil,' insisted the voice.

'Phil, where are you?'

'In heaven,' replied Phil. 'I have some really good news and a little bad news.'

'Tell me the good news first,' said Joe.

'The good news,' Phil said with joy and enthusiasm, 'is that there is baseball in heaven. Better yet, all of our old buddies who died before me are here, too. Even better than that, we're all young again. Better still, it's always springtime and it never rains or snows. And best of all, we can play ball all we want, and we never get tired. And we get to play with all the Greats of the past.'

'That's fantastic,' said Joe 'It's beyond my wildest dreams! So what's the bad news?'

'You're pitching Tuesday.'

I think the life cycle is backwards:

You should start out dead and thus get it out of the way. Then, you wake up in an old folks' home, feeling better every day. You get kicked out for being too healthy; go collect your pension, then when you start work, you get a gold watch on your first day.

You work 40 years until you're young enough to enjoy your retirement. You drink alcohol, you party, you're generally promiscuous, you then get ready for University, then Secondary School. You go to Primary school, you become a kid, you play, you have no responsibilities, you become a baby, and then... You spend your last nine months floating peacefully in luxury, in spa-like conditions, with central heating, room service on tap, larger quarters to live in every day.

And then you finish off as an orgasm. What a way to go!

New wine:

I heard it through the grapevine that Clare Valley vintners in South Australia, which primarily produce Pinot Blanc, Pinot Noir, and Pinot Grigio wines, have developed a new hybrid grape that acts as an anti-diuretic. It is expected to reduce the number of trips older people have to make to the bathroom during the night.

The new wine will be marketed as Pino More.

Older people's brains:

Brains of older people are slow because they know so much. People do not decline mentally with age, it just takes them longer to recall facts because they have more information in their brains, scientists believe. Much like a computer struggles as the hard drive gets full, so, too, do humans take longer to access information when their brains are full.

Researchers say this slowing down process is not the same as cognitive decline. The human brain works slower in old age, said Dr. Michael Ramscar, but only because we have stored more information over time. The brains of older people do not get weak. On the contrary, they simply know more.

Also, older people often go to another room to get something and when they get there, they stand there wondering what they came for. It is NOT a memory problem; it is nature's way of making older people do more exercise.

Now when I reach for a word or a name, I won't excuse myself by saying 'I'm having a senior moment.' Now, I'll say, 'My disk is full!'

I have more friends I should send this to, but right now I can't remember their names. So, please forward this to your friends; they may be my friends, too.

At the theatre:

An old man lay sprawled across three entire seats at a concert. When the usher came by and noticed this, he whispered to the old man, 'Sorry sir, but you're only allowed one seat.'

The old man didn't budge. The usher became more impatient. 'Sir, if you don't get up from there I'm going to have to call the manager.'

Once again, the old man just muttered and did nothing. The usher marched briskly back up the aisle, and in a moment he returned with the manager. Together the two of them tried repeatedly to move the old dishevelled man, but with no success.

Finally, they summoned the police. The officer surveyed the situation briefly then asked, 'All right buddy what's your name?'

'Fred,' the old man moaned.

'Where you from, Fred?' asked the police officer.

With a terrible strain in his voice, and without moving, Fred replied; 'The balcony.

Jokes for older folks:

- Man sitting on the side of his bed says, 'Yipee! I woke up! (Why retirees are always so happy.)
- Since it was such a crappy day I sat in my recliner and started thinking about life and came to realize that as I've grown older I've learned that pleasing everyone is impossible, but pissing everyone off is a piece of cake.
- Condoms don't guarantee safe sex any more, a friend of mine was wearing one when he was shot by the woman's husband.
- Drive -by… Someone broke into my house last week. They didn't take my TV - just the remote. Now they drive by and change the channels. The Sick bastards!
- The Agony of Aging… On the morning that Daylight Savings Time ended I stopped in to visit my aging friend. He was busy covering his penis with black shoe polish. I said to him, 'You'd better get your hearing checked - You're supposed to turn your clock back.'
- Video Scam… Just got scammed out of $25. Bought Tiger Woods DVD entitled 'My Favourite 18 Holes.' Turns out it's all about golf. Absolute waste of money! Pass this on so others don't get scammed.
- Pregnant Prostitute… Doctor asks a pregnant prostitute, 'Do you know who the father is?'
Hey dumb ass,' she replied, 'if you ate a can of beans would you know which one made you fart?'
- At barbers: Express cut – 20 hairs or less.
- When I get old, I'm going to move in with my kids, hog the computer, pay no bills, eat all the food, trash the house, and when asked to clean, pitch a fit like it's killing me.
- Of course I talk to myself. Sometimes I need expert advice.

- Aging seems to be the only available way to have a longer life.
- When I die, I want my last words to be, 'I left a million dollars under the...'
- I really think that tossing and turning at night should be considered as exercise.
- I've reached the age when my train of thought often leaves the station without me.
- Enjoy life – it has an expiration date.
- Madonna is 55 – her boyfriend is 22. Tina Turner is 75 – her boyfriend is 40; JLo is 42, her boyfriend is 32. Still single? Relax – your boyfriend isn't even born yet.
- We're all mature until someone brings out bubble wrap.
- Some people just need a pat on the head – with a hammer.
- Yet another day has gone by, and I haven't had to use algebra once.
- I have a brain like the Bermuda Triangle – info goes in, never to be found again.
- Scene: An elderly gentleman draws up to a post box and says, 'I'll have a cheeseburger, large fries and black coffee.
  Bystander tells friend, 'I'm beginning to think that re-testing seniors for driving isn't a bad idea.'
- Woman at the 'Autumn Years Dating Agency' to older woman, 'It says here that you'd prefer someone with regular bowel movements. Does it matter if they're involuntary?'
- Older woman to another older woman, 'Lately, I've been feeling lethargic, listless and apathetic, and if I stand up too suddenly, I get dizzy. My daughter says she has to smoke two joints to feel like that!'
- Wife to elderly husband, 'You don't look anything like the long-haired, skinny kid I married 25 years ago. I need a DNA sample to make sure it's still you.'
- Young woman at the photo copying centre to older lady, 'I hope you don't mind, but I used the computer to

remove all those age spots, wrinkles and that hideous mole you have on your chin.'
- Older woman to another older woman, 'I'm getting so old that all my friends in heaven will think I didn't make it.'
- Older man says, 'My wild oats have turned into prunes and All Bran.'
- Woman sitting in bed next to her slumbering husband, 'Hey wake up. The cat's got your teeth.'
- I'm going to retire and live off my savings. What I'll do the second day, I have no idea.
- All you young whipper-snappers will never know the pleasure and satisfaction you can have by slamming down the phone on an old-type phone.
- I believe my house is haunted. Every time I look in the mirror – a crazy old lady stands in front of me so I can't see my reflection!
- He: The internet is so fascinating!
  She: You dope – that's the microwave!
- I really think that tossing and turning at night should be considered as exercise
- Do you remember when you used to refer to your knees as right and left – not it's good and bad.
- Push – if that doesn't work – Pull! If that doesn't work – we're closed.
- You know you're getting old when you can't walk past a washroom without thinking, 'I may as well pee while I'm here.'
- Don't stress about your eyesight failing as we get older, It's nature's way of protecting us from shock when we pass a mirror.
- I've decided on a new career. I'm going to be a backwards stripper. I'll come out on the stage naked and they will pay me to put my clothes back on.
- Don't get your meds mixed up. Yesterday I put Preparation 'H' on my dentures instead of 'Poli-Grip.' Now I talk like an asshole, but my gums don't itch.

- The scariest feeling in the world is the split second when you lose your balance in the shower and think, 'Oh God! They're going to find me naked and without my teeth!'
- If there are no ups and downs in your life – you're dead!
- It's your road and yours alone – others may walk it with you, but no one can walk it for you.
- In the end, we may regret the chances we didn't take, relationships we were afraid to have and the decisions we waited too long to make.
- Inside every older person is a younger person wondering what the hell happened!
- I don't want to say I'm old and worn out, but I make sure I'm nowhere near the curb on garbage day.
- Young girls are made of sugar and spice and everything nice. I must be made of wine and caffeine and everything mean – because that's what old broads are made of.
- You know you're old when you wake up with that awful 'morning after' feeling… and you didn't do anything the night before.
- Aging gracefully is just a tactful way of saying you're slowly looking worse.
- I need to get in shape. If I was murdered tonight, my chalk outline would be a circle.
- Story of my life: I knew better; but I did it anyway.
- **Sometimes the grass will appear greener on the other side because it was fertilized by bullshit.**
- The truth doesn't cost anything, but a lie could cost you everything.

Pathology tests:

The phone rings and the lady of the house answers. 'Hello?'

'Mrs. Sanders, please.'

'Speaking.'

'Mrs. Sanders, this is Dr. Jones at St. Agnes Laboratory. When your husband's doctor sent his biopsy to the lab last week, a biopsy from another Mr. Sanders arrived as well. We are now uncertain which one belongs to your husband. Frankly, either way the results are not too good.'

'What do you mean?' Mrs. Sanders asks nervously.

'Well, one of the specimens tested positive for Alzheimer's and the other one tested positive for HIV. We can't tell which is which.'

'That's dreadful! Can you do the test again?' questioned Mrs. Sanders.

'Normally we could have; but the new government health care system will only pay for these expensive tests just one time.'

'Well, what am I supposed to do now?'

'The folks at OHIP recommend that you drop your husband off, somewhere in the middle of town. If he finds his way home, don't sleep with him.'

A new year:

Another year has passed
And we're all a little older.
Last summer felt hotter
And winter seems much colder.
There was a time not long ago
When life was quite a blast.
Now I fully understand
About 'Living in the Past'
We used to go to weddings,
Football games and lunches.
Now we go to funeral homes
And after-funeral brunches.
We used to have hangovers,
From parties that were gay.
Now we suffer body aches

And while the night away.
We used to go out dining,
And couldn't get our fill.
Now we ask for doggie bags,
Come home and take a pill.
We used to often travel
To places near and far.
Now we get sore asses
From riding in the car.
We used to go to nightclubs
And drink a little booze.
Now we stay home at night
And watch the evening news.
That, my friend is how life is,
And now my tale is told.
So, enjoy each day and live it up
Before you're too damned old!

CHAPTER 10

BLONDE JOKES

Two blondes walked into a building. You'd think at least one of them would have seen it.

Redecorating:

A blonde decided to redecorate her bedroom. She wasn't sure how many rolls of wallpaper she would need, but she knew that her blonde friend from next door had recently done the same job and the two rooms were identical in size.

'Buffy,' she said, 'How many rolls of wallpaper did you buy for your bedroom?'

'Ten, said Buffy.

So the blonde bought the ten rolls of paper and did the job, but she had two rolls left over.

'Buffy,' she said. 'I bought ten rolls of wallpaper for the bedroom, but I've got two left over.'

'Yes.' said Buffy. 'So did I.'

One eye:

Two blondes were walking down the road when the first blonde said, 'Look at that dog with one eye!'

The other blonde covers one of her eyes and says, 'Where?'

Two blondes were filling up at a gas station and the first blonde said to the second, 'I'll bet these awful gas prices are going to go even higher.'

The second blonde replies, 'Won't affect me – I always put in just $15 worth.'

Pet python:

A blonde was selling her pet Python on eBay. A fellow called up and asked if it was big.

She said, 'It's massive.'

He said, 'How many feet?'

She replied, 'None. Are you nuts - it's a snake.'

Grandma's advice

Grandma to blonde granddaughter, 'Dear, if you're going to pad your bra with tissue, you need to take them out of the box first.'

Stay:

I pulled into the crowded parking lot at the local shopping centre and rolled down the car windows to make sure my Labrador Retriever Pup had fresh air.

She was stretched full-out on the back seat and I wanted to impress upon her that she must remain there.

I walked to the curb backward, pointing my finger at the car and saying emphatically, 'Now you stay. Do you hear me? Stay! Stay!'

The driver of a nearby car, a pretty young blonde, gave me a strange look and said, 'Why don't you just put it in 'Park'?'

2015 - A Blonde's year in review:

January: Took new scarf back to store because it was too tight.

February: Fired from pharmacy job for failing to print labels. Helllloooo!!! Bottles won't fit in printer!!!

March: Got really excited... finished jigsaw puzzle in 6 months. Box said ' 2-4 years!'

April: Trapped on escalator for hours. Power went out!

May: Tried to make Jungle Juice - wrong instructions... 8 cups of water won't fit into those little packets!

June: Tried to go water skiing... Couldn't find a lake with a slope.

July: Lost breast stroke swimming competition... Learned later that the other swimmers cheated- they used their arms!

August: Got locked out of my car in rain storm... Darn car filled up with water because convertible top was open.

September: The capital of California is 'C'... isn't it?

October: I hate M & M's...They're so hard to peel.

November Baked Thanksgiving turkey for 4 1/2 days... Instructions said bake 1 hour per pound and I weigh 108!

December: Couldn't call 911. 'Duh'... there's no 'eleven' button on the stupid phone!

CHAPTER 11

RELIGIOUS JOKES

Jewish modesty:

A Catholic, a Protestant, a Muslim and a Jew were in a discussion during a dinner.

Catholic, 'I have a large fortune. I'm going to buy Citibank.'

Protestant, 'I'm very wealthy and I will buy General Motors.'

Muslim, 'I'm a fabulously rich prince. I intend to purchase Microsoft.

They then all wait for the Jew to speak. The Jew stirs his coffee, places the spoon neatly on the table, takes a sip of his coffee, looks at them and casually says, 'I'm not selling.'

Doing without:

God visited a woman and told her she must give up smoking, drinking and sex if she wants to get into heaven. The woman said she would try her best.

God visited the woman a week later to see how she was getting on. 'Not bad,'

Said the woman, 'I've given up smoking and drinking but when I bent over the lounge suite, my boyfriend caught sight of my long slender legs and made love to me right then and there.'

'They don't like that in heaven,' said God

The woman replied: 'They're not too happy about it at Harvey Norman either!'

Picnic:

A Jewish Rabbi and a Catholic Priest met at the town's annual 4th of July picnic. Old friends, they began their usual banter.

'This baked ham is really delicious,' the priest teased the rabbi. 'You really ought to try it. I know it's against your religion, but I can't understand why such a wonderful food should be forbidden! You don't know what you're missing. You just haven't lived until you've tried Mrs. Hall's prized Virginia Baked Ham. Tell me Rabbi, when are you going to break down and try it?'

The rabbi looked at the priest with a big grin, and said, 'At your wedding.'

Forgive me.

A veteran enters the Catholic Church confessional booth and tells the priest, 'Bless me Father, for I have sinned. Last night, I beat the ever-living daylights out of a flag-burning, cop-hating, terrorist.'

The priest said, 'My son, I'm here to forgive your sins, not to discuss your community service.'

Who's the boss?

In heaven God told all husbands and wives to gather for a meeting! He told the men to stand in two queues; those who are controlled by their wives and those who control their wives!

Only one man stood in the second queue.

God said 'So you control your wife?'

Man: 'Are you crazy? My wife told me to stand here.'

Counting blessings:

Today, on a bus, I saw a very beautiful woman and wished I were as beautiful. When suddenly she rose to leave, I saw her hobble down the aisle. She had one leg and used a crutch. But as she passed, she passed a smile. 'Oh, God, forgive me when I whine. I have two legs; the world is mine.'

I stopped to buy some candy. The lad who sold it had such charm. I talked with him, he seemed so glad. If I were late, it'd do no harm. And as I left, he said to me, 'I thank you, you've been so kind. It's nice to talk with folks like you. You see,' he said, 'I'm blind.' Oh, God, forgive me when I whine. I have two eyes; the world is mine.'

Later while walking down the street, I saw a child I knew. He stood and watched the others play, but he did not know what to do. I stopped a moment and then I said, 'Why don't you join them dear?'

He looked ahead without a word. I forgot, he couldn't hear. 'Oh, God, forgive me when I whine. I have two ears; the world is mine.'

'With feet to take me where I'd go; with eyes to see the sunset's glow; with ears to hear what I'd know; Oh, God, forgive me when I whine. I've been blessed; indeed, the world is mine.

Her title:

The Bishop of St. Asaph and his wife were on holiday in Spain and were just signing in to their hotel in Seville. Although bishops of the Church in Wales have a title; their wives are known as 'Mrs.' So the good prelate wrote in the register: The Bishop of St Asaph and Mrs. Williams.

The hotel manager looked at the register in amazement and taking the Bishop to one side said, 'In Spain, Bishop, we are not as is commonly said, narrow-minded, and it is no concern of mine what your relationship is with this woman, but do you not think you could conduct this affair a little more discreetly?'

Walk again:

From now on, I believe in the Prophet Muhammed. I decided to go to the local mosque for the first time to see what it was all about. I sat down and Imam came up to me, laid his hands on my hand and said, 'By the will of Allah and the prophet Muhammed, you will walk today.'

I told him I wasn't paralysed – I only had a small bunion on my left foot. He came back and laid his hands on me and looking skywards, earnestly repeated his mantra, 'By the will of Allah and the prophet Muhammed, you will walk today.'

Once again, I told him there was nothing wrong with me. After prayers I stepped outside – and bugger me – my car was gone!

The gift:

Sitting by the window of her convent, Sister Barbara opened a letter from home one evening. Inside the letter was a $100 note her parents had sent. Sister Barbara smiled at the gesture. As she read the letter by the window she noticed a shabbily dressed stranger leaning against the light pole below.

Quickly, she wrote, 'Don't despair – Sister Barbara' on a piece of paper and wrapped the $100 in it. She got the man's attention and tossed it out the window to him. The stranger picked it up and with a puzzled expression and tip of his hat, went off down the street.

The next day, Sister Barbara was told that a man was at the gate insisting on seeing her. She went out and found the stranger waiting. Without a word he handed her a huge wad of $100 notes.

'What's this?' she asked.

'That's the $8,000 you have owing to you Sister,' he replied. 'Don't Despair came in 80 to 1.'

Differing viewpoints:

A 17-year-old boy was shopping in a sports store. The cashier was a Muslim lady who was wearing her headscarf. The 17-year-old was wearing a necklace with a cross on it. She told him he would have to put his cross under his shirt because it offended her. He told her he would not do that.

Then he told her that he thought she should take her headscarf off because it offended him. She called for the manager.

The manager told the 17-year-old to just put his cross under his shirt and everything would be fine. The boy again refused to do so and at that point he left the items he had intended to purchase and walked out.

Several customers who had been in line behind him had heard the conversation and also left their carts full of items and walked out of the store.

We all know we are living in some very changing times, and given the same circumstances, I pray we would all have the courage this young lad had.

At the ball game:

Three nuns were attending a Yankee baseball game. Three men were sitting directly behind them. Because their habits were partially blocking the view, the men decided to badger the nuns hoping that they'd get annoyed enough to move to another area.

In a very loud voice, the first guy said, 'I think I'm going to move to Utah. There are only 100 nuns living there.'

Then the second guy spoke up and said, 'I want to go to Montana. There are only 5o nuns living there.'

The third guy said, 'I want to go to Idaho. There are only 25 nuns living there.'

The mother superior turned around, looked at the men, and in a very sweet and calm voice said,

'Why don't you go to hell... There aren't any nuns there!'

Time to get up:

One Sunday morning, a mother went in to wake her son and tell him it was time to get ready for church, to which he replied, 'I'm not going.'

'Why not?' she asked.

'I'll give you two good reasons,' he said, 'One, they don't like me, and two, I don't like them.'

His mother replied, 'I'll give you two good reasons why you *should* go to church: One – you're 59 years old and two – you're the pastor!'

Goat for dinner:

A young couple invited their elderly pastor for Sunday dinner. While they were in the kitchen preparing the meal, the minister asked their son what they were having for dinner.

'Goat,' the little boy replied.

'Goat?' replied the startled man of the cloth, 'Are you sure about that?'

'Yep,' said the youngster, 'I heard Dad say to Mom, 'Today is just as good as any to have the old goat for dinner.'

Out of the mouths of the babes:

I certainly don't think an adult could explain this more beautifully! It was written by an 8-year-old named Danny Dutton, who lives in Chula Vista, CA. He wrote it for his third-grade homework assignment, to explain God. I wonder if any of us could have done as well?

'One of God's main jobs is making people. He makes them to replace the ones that die, so there will be enough people to take care of things on earth. He doesn't make grownups, just babies. I think because they are smaller and easier to make. That way he doesn't have to take up his valuable time teaching them to talk and walk. He can just leave that to mothers and fathers.'

'God's second most important job is listening to prayers. An awful lot of this goes on, since some people, like preachers and things, pray at times beside bedtime. God doesn't have time to listen to the radio or TV because of this. Because he hears everything, there must be a terrible lot of noise in his ears, unless he has thought of a way to turn it off.'

'God sees everything and hears everything and is everywhere which keeps Him pretty busy. So you shouldn't go wasting his time by going over your mom and dad's head asking for something they said you couldn't have.'

'Atheists are people who don't believe in God. I don't think there are any in Chula Vista. At least there aren't any who come to our church.'

'Jesus is God's Son. He used to do all the hard work, like walking on water and performing miracles and trying to teach the people who didn't want to learn about God. They finally got tired of him preaching to them and they crucified him. But he was good and kind, like his father, and he told his father that they didn't know what they were doing and to forgive them and God said okay.'

'His dad (God) appreciated everything that he had done and all his hard work on earth so he told him he didn't have to go out on the road anymore. He could stay in heaven. So he did. And now he helps his dad out by listening to prayers and seeing things which are important for God to take care of and which ones he can take care of himself without having to bother God. Like a secretary, only more important.'

'You can pray anytime you want and they are sure to help you because they got it worked out so one of them is on duty all the time.'

'You should always go to church on Sunday because it makes God happy, and if there's anybody you want to make happy, it's God!

Don't skip church to do something you think will be more fun like going to the beach. This is wrong. And besides the sun doesn't come out at the beach until noon anyway.'

'If you don't believe in God, besides being an atheist, you will be very lonely, because your parents can't go everywhere with you, like to camp, but God can. It is good to know He's around you when you're scared, in the dark or when you can't swim and you get thrown into real deep water by big kids.'

'But... you shouldn't just always think of what God can do for you. I figure God put me here and he can take me back anytime he pleases. And... that's why I believe in God.'

Making a call:

A man in Hell asked the Devil, 'Can I make a call to my wife?'

After making the call he asked how much he had to pay. The Devil replied, 'Nothing, in-house calls are free.'

Catholic Saint:

There is a Catholic Saint of Beer. Saint Arnold of Soissons saved the lives of many by urging them to drink beer rather than water that was spreading the plague. Boiling during the brewing process killed the pathogens.

Can you get married in heaven?

On their way to get married, a young Catholic couple is involved in a fatal car accident. The couple find themselves sitting outside the Pearly Gates waiting for St. Peter to process them into Heaven. While waiting, they begin to wonder: Could they possibly get married in Heaven? When St. Peter shows up, they asked him.

St. Peter says, 'I don't know. This is the first time anyone has asked. Let me go find out,' and he leaves.

The couple sat and waited, and waited. Two months passed and the couple are still waiting. As they waited, they discussed that if they were allowed to get married in Heaven, what was the eternal aspect of it all. 'What if it doesn't work?' they wondered, 'Are we stuck together forever?' After yet another month, St. Peter finally returns, looking somewhat bedraggled. 'Yes,' he informs the couple, 'you can get married in Heaven.'

'Great!' said the couple, 'but we were just wondering, what if things don't work out? Could we also get a divorce in Heaven?'

St. Peter, red-faced with anger, slammed his clipboard onto the ground.

'What's wrong?' asked the frightened couple.

'Oh, come on!', St. Peter shouted, 'It took me three months to find a priest up here! Do you have any idea how long it'll take me to find a lawyer?!'

Gotcha:

Father O'Malley rose from his bed one morning. It was a fine spring day in his new parish. He walked to the window of his bedroom to get a deep breath of the beautiful day outside. He then noticed there was a donkey lying dead in the middle of his front lawn. He promptly called the local police station.

The conversation went like this: 'Good morning. This is Sergeant Jones. How might I help you?'

'And the best of the day te yerself. This is Father O'Malley at St. Ann's Catholic Church. There's a donkey lying dead in me front lawn and would ye be so kind as to send a couple o'yer lads to take care of the matter?'

Sergeant Jones, considering himself to be quite a wit and recognizing the Irish accent, thought he would have a little fun with the good father, replied, 'Well now Father, it was always my impression that you people took care of the last rites!'

There was dead silence on the line for a moment then Father O'Malley replied: 'Aye,' tis certainly true; but we are also obliged to notify the next of kin first, which is the reason for me call.'

Holy humour:

A father was approached by his small son who told him proudly, 'I know what the Bible means!'

His father smiled and replied, 'What do you mean, you 'know' what the Bible means?'

The son replied, 'I do know!'

'Okay,' said his father. 'What does the Bible mean?'

'That's easy, Daddy...' the young boy replied excitedly, 'It stands for 'Basic Information Before Leaving Earth.'

There was a very gracious lady who was mailing an old family Bible to her brother in another part of the country.

'Is there anything breakable in here?' asked the postal clerk.

'Only the Ten Commandments.' answered the lady.

'Somebody has said there are only two kinds of people in the world. There are those who wake up in the morning and say, 'Good morning, Lord,' and there are those who wake up in the morning and say, 'Good Lord, its morning.'

A minister parked his car in a no-parking zone in a large city because he was short of time and couldn't find a space with a meter. Then he put a note under the windshield wiper that read: 'I have circled the block ten times. If I don't park here, I'll miss my appointment. Forgive us our trespasses.'

When he returned, he found a citation from a police officer along with this note 'I've circled this block for 10 years. If I don't give you a ticket, I'll lose my job.

While driving in Pennsylvania, a family caught up to an Amish carriage. The owner of the carriage obviously had a sense of humour, because attached to the back of the carriage was a hand printed sign... 'Energy efficient vehicle: Runs on oats and grass. Caution: Do not step in exhaust.'

People want the front of the bus, the back of the church, and the centre of attention.

The minister was preoccupied with thoughts of how he was going to ask the congregation to come up with more money than they were expecting for repairs to the church building. Therefore, he was annoyed to find that the regular organist was sick and a substitute had been brought in at the last minute. The substitute wanted to know what to play.

'Here's a copy of the service,' he said impatiently. 'But, you'll have to think of something to play after I make the announcement about the finances.'

During the service, the minister paused and said, 'Brothers and Sisters, we are in great difficulty; the roof repairs cost twice as much as we expected and we need $4,000 more.

Any of you who can pledge $100 or more, please stand up.'

At that moment, the substitute organist played 'The Star Spangled Banner.'

And that is how the substitute became the regular organist!

Six months more:

Three Italian Nuns die and go to heaven. At the Pearly Gates, they are met by St. Peter. He said, 'Sisters, you have all led such exemplary lives that The Lord is granting you six months to go back to Earth to live the life of anyone you wish to be.'

The first nun said, 'I want to be Sophia Loren; she's a lovely lady and a great Italian woman and role model' And *poof* she was gone.

The second said, 'I want to be Madonna. Although sometimes controversial - she's a great entertainer.' And *poof* she was gone.

The third said, 'I want to be Sarah Pipalini'

St. Peter looking confused asked, 'Who?'

'Sarah Pipalini,' repeated the nun.

St. Peter shook his head and said, 'I'm sorry, but that name doesn't ring a bell.'

The nun then takes a newspaper out of her habit and hands it to St. Peter. St. Peter reads the paper and starts laughing. He hands it back to her and says. 'No sister. The paper says it was the 'Sahara Pipeline' that was laid by 1,400 men in 6 months.'

[If you laughed, you're going straight to hell!]

Groom not welcome:

Nancy was Catholic, but her fiancé, Chris, was not. Since my friends were planning to be married in the Catholic Church, Chris made sure to listen carefully throughout their prenuptial sessions. At one meeting the priest turned to Chris and told him, 'Since you are not Catholic, we shall have the ceremony without Eucharist.'

Later that day, Chris was noticeably upset, so Nancy asked what was wrong. 'I don't understand,' he said. 'How can we have the ceremony without me?'

CHAPTER 12

AT WORK

On the sport scene:

I think it's just terrible how everyone has treated Lance Armstrong, especially after what he achieved, winning seven Tour de France races while on drugs. When I was on drugs, I couldn't even find my bike.

The interview:

The executive was interviewing a young blonde for a position in his company. He wanted to find out something about her personality so he asked, 'If you could have a conversation with any person, living or dead – who would that be?'

The blonde quickly responded, 'The living one.'

Customer Service:

Prices subject to change according to customer's attitude.

Was fired:

'I got fired today!' I told my mate, 'for downloading dirty pictures on the work computer and causing everything to crash.'

'That's a bit harsh,' his friend replied.

'Well, they don't muck around at Air Traffic Control,' I said.

Not feeling well:

Patti was doing some roofing work for Murphy., As he nears the top of the ladder he starts shaking and feeling dizzy. He called down to Murphy, 'I tink I will ave to go home. I've come all over tiddy and feel sick.'

Murphy asks, 'Ave yer got vertigo?'

Paddy replies, 'No I only live round the corner.'

Accounting problem:

The owner of a golf course was confused about paying an invoice, so he decided to ask his secretary for some mathematical assistance. He called her into his office and said, 'You graduated from university and I need some help. If I were to give you $20,000 minus 14%, how much would you take off?'

The secretary thought for a moment and then replied, 'Everything but my earrings.'

Job interviews:

An Italian, French and Chinese went for a job interview in England. Before the interview, they were told they must compose a sentence in English with three main words: green, pink and yellow.

The Italian was first: 'I wake up in the morning. I see the yellow sun. I see the green grass and I think to myself, 'I hope it will be a pink day.''

The French was next: 'I wake up in the morning. I eat a yellow banana, a green pepper and in the evening I watch the Pink Panther on TV.

The Chinese was the last: 'I wake up in the morning. I hear the phone 'green green.' I 'pink' up the phone and I say, 'yellow!!'

Winking

A man with a winking problem is applying for a position as a sales representative for a large firm. The interviewer looks over his papers and says, 'This is phenomenal, you've graduated from the best schools; your recommendations are wonderful, and your experience is unparalleled. Normally, we'd hire you without a second thought. However, a sales representative has a highly visible position, and we're afraid that your constant winking will scare off potential customers. I'm sorry... we can't hire you.'

'But wait,' the man says. 'if I take two aspirin, I'll stop winking!'

'Really? Great! Show me now!'

So the applicant reaches into his jacket pocket and begins pulling out all sorts of condoms; red condoms, blue condoms, ribbed condoms, flavoured condoms; finally, at the bottom, he finds a packet of aspirin. He tears it open, swallows the pills, and stops winking.

'Well,' said the interviewer, 'that's all well and good, but this is a respectable company, and we will not have our employees womanizing all over the country!'

'Womanizing? What do you mean? I'm a happily married man!'

'Well then, how do you explain all these condoms?'

'Oh, that,' he sighed. 'Have you ever walked into a pharmacy, winking, and asked for a packet of aspirin?'

Basic English:

At the final dinner of an international conference, and American delegate turned to the Chinese delegate sitting next to him – pointed to the soup and asked somewhat condescendingly, 'Likee soupee?'

The Chinese gentleman nodded eagerly. A little later it was, 'Likee fishee? And 'Likee meatee" and 'Liokee frutee" and always the response was an affable nod.

At the end of the dinner the chairman of the conference introduced the guest speaker of the evening: none other than the Chinese gentleman who delivered a penetrating, witty discourse in impeccable English, much to the astonishment of his American neighbour.

When the speech was over, the speaker turned to his neighbour and with a mischievous twinkle in his eye asked, 'Likee speechee?"

Wine taster:

At a winery, the regular taster died and the director started looking for a new one to hire. A drunkard with a ragged, dirty look came in to apply for the position. The director of the winery wondered how to send him away. He gave him a glass to drink. The drunk tried it and said, 'It's a Muscat, three years old, grown on a north slope, matured in steel containers. Low grade, but acceptable.'

'That's correct,' said the boss.

He gave the man another glass.

'This is a Cabernet, eight years old, a south-western slope, oak barrels, matured at 8 degrees. Requires three more years for finest results.'

'Correct.' And gave him a third glass.

'It's a Pinot Blanc Champagne, high grade and exclusive," the drunk said calmly.

The director was astonished. He winked at his secretary, secretly suggesting something. She left the room, and came back in with a glass of urine. The alcoholic tried it.

'It's a blonde, 26 years old, three months pregnant and if I don't get the job I'll name the father.'

P.S. You know you're a wine nerd so when you read this, your initial reaction was 'But there's almost no such thing as Pinot Blanc Champagne any more and the few still-existing Pinot Blanc plantings in Champagne vineyards can't be replanted or expanded under AOC designation.'

Wal-Mart Greeter:

Young people forget that we old people had a career before we retired. Charley, a new retiree-greeter at Wal-Mart, just couldn't seem to get to work on time. Every day he was 5, 10, 15 minutes late. But he was a good worker, really tidy, clean-shaven, sharp-minded and a real credit to the company and obviously demonstrating their 'Older Person Friendly' policies.

One day the boss called him into the office for a talk. 'Charley, I have to tell you, I like your work ethic, you do a bang-up job when you finally get here; but you being late so often is quite bothersome.'

'Yes, I know boss and I am sorry and am working on it.'

'Well good, you are a team player. That's what I like to hear.'

'Yes sir, I understand your concern and I will try harder.'

Seeming puzzled, the manager went on to comment, 'I know you're retired from the Armed Forces. What did they say to you there if you showed up in the morning late so often?'

The old man looked down at the floor, then smiled. He chuckled quietly, then said with a grin,

'They usually saluted and said, Good morning, Admiral, can I get your coffee, sir?'

Wrong number:

A junior in the office dialled his boss's extension by mistake and said: 'Hey, send a coffee to my office in two minutes.'

The boss shouted: 'Do you know who you are talking to?'

Junior: 'No!'

Boss: 'I'm the boss!'

Junior (in same tone): 'Do you know whom you are talking to?'

Boss: 'No!'

Junior: 'Thank goodness for that!'

Mathematics:

This comes from two math teachers with a combined total of 70 years' experience. It has an indisputable mathematical logic. It also made me laugh out loud. This is a strictly mathematical viewpoint and it goes like this:

What makes 100%? What does it mean to give MORE than 100%?

Ever wonder about those people who say they are giving more than 100%? We have all been to those meetings where someone wants you to give over 100%. How about achieving 103%? What makes up 100% in life?

Here's a little mathematical formula that might help you answer these questions:

If: A B C D E F G H I J K L M N O P Q R S T U V W X Y Z

Is represented as: 1 2 3 4 5 6 7 8 9 10 11 12 13 14 15 16 17 18 19 20 21 22 23 24 25 26.

Then:

H-A-R-D-W-O-R-K: 8+1+18+4+23+15+18+11 = 98%

And

K-N-O-W-L-E-D-G-E: 11+14+15+23+12+5+4+7+5 = 96%

But,

A-T-T-I-T-U-D-E: 1+20+20+9+20+21+4+5 = 100%

And,

B-U-L-L-S-H-I-T: 2+21+12+12+19+8+9+20 = 103%

And, look how far ass-kissing will take you.

A-S-S-K-I-S-S-I-N-G: 1+19+19+11+9+19+19+9+14+7 = 127%

So, one can conclude with mathematical certainty, that while Hard Work and Knowledge will get you close, and Attitude will get you there. It's the Bullshit and Ass-Kissing that will put you over the top.

Now you know why some people are where they are. I've never seen a better explanation than this formula. How true it is.

The flagpole:

Raymond and Bubba, two government mechanical engineers, were standing at the base of a flagpole, looking up. A woman walked by and asked what they were doing.

'We're supposed to find the height of the flagpole,' said Bubba, 'but we don't have a ladder.'

The woman said, 'Hand me that wrench out of your toolbox.'

She loosened a few bolts, and laid the pole down. Then she took a tape measure from their toolbox, took a measurement, and announced, 'Eighteen feet, six inches,' and walked away.

Raymond shook his head and laughed. 'Ain't that just like a Miss know-it-all woman! We ask for the height and she gives us the length!'

Bubba and Ray are still working for the government.

Logger:

Rangi (who's not very swift in the brain department) gets a job felling trees in the North of Canada. At the end of his first day, the foreman comes to check on his work. Rangi has felled only one tree.

'What the hell's going on here, Rangi? Only one tree felled in a day.'

Rangi says, 'This bloody saw's no good boss. Doesn't cut at all.'

The boss says, 'Here, let me try.'

He starts up the chainsaw. Rangi looks startled. 'What's that noise, boss?'

The funniest staff meeting ever:

The boss of a Madison Avenue advertising agency called a spontaneous staff meeting in the middle of a particularly stressful week. (This is one pretty sharp boss!) When everyone gathered, the boss, who understood the benefits of having fun, told the burnt out staff the purpose of the meeting was to have a quick contest.

The theme: Viagra advertising slogans. The only rule was they had to use past ad slogans, originally written for other products that captured the essence of Viagra. Slight variations were acceptable.

About 7 minutes later, they turned in their suggestions and created a Top 10 List. With all the laughter and camaraderie, the rest of the week went very well for everyone!

The top 10 were:

10. Viagra, Whaazzzz up!

9. Viagra, The quicker pecker upper.

8. Viagra, like a rock!

7. Viagra, when it absolutely, positively has to be there overnight.

6. Viagra, be all that you can be.

5. Viagra, Reach out and touch someone.

4. Viagra, Strong enough for a man, but made for a woman.

3. Viagra, Home of the whopper!

2. Viagra, we bring good things to Life!

And the unanimous number one slogan:

1. This is your peepee. This is your peepee on drugs.

Murphy the Irish painter:

A painter by the name of Murphy, while not a brilliant scholar, was a gifted portrait artist. Over a short number of years, his fame grew and soon people from all over Ireland were coming to the town of Miltown Malbay, in County Clare, to get him to paint their likenesses.

One day, a beautiful young English woman arrived at his house in a stretch limo and asked if he would paint her in the nude. This being the first time anyone had made such a request he was a bit perturbed, particularly when the woman told him that money was no object; in fact, and she was willing to pay up to £10,000.

Not wanting to get into any marital strife, he asked her to wait while he went into the house to confer with Mary, his wife. They talked much about the rightness and wrongness of it. It was hard to make the decision but finally his wife agreed, on one condition.

In a few minutes he returned. 'T'would be me pleasure to paint yer portrait, missus,' he said 'The wife says it's okay. I'll paint you in the nude all right; but I have to at least leave me socks on, so I have a place to wipe me brushes.'

Parallels:

Paradise would be a place where everybody has guaranteed employment, free comprehensive healthcare, free education, free food, free housing, free clothing, free utilities, and only law enforcement has guns. And believe it or not, such a place does indeed already exist: It's called Prison.

Benefits of the following:

Prison - You spend most of your time in a 10X10 cell.
At Work – You spend most of your time in a 6X6 cell.

Prison – You get three meals a day, fully paid for.

At Work – You get a break for one meal and you have to pay for it.

Prison – For good behaviour – you get time off.
At Work – For good behaviour – you get more work.

Prison – The guard locks and unlocks all the doors for you.
At Home - You must carry a security card and open all the doors yourself.

Prison – You can watch TV and play games.
At Home – You could get fired for watching TV and playing games.

Prison – You get your own toilet.
At Work – You have to share the toilet with people who pee on the seat.

Prison – They allow your family and friends to visit.
At Work – You aren't even supposed to speak to your family.

Prison – All expenses are paid by taxpayers with no work required.
At Work – You must pay all your expenses to go to work and they deduct extras from your salary to pay for prisoners.

Prison – You spend most of your life inside bars waiting to get out.
At Work – You spend most of your time wanting to get out and go inside bars.

Prison – You must deal with sadistic wardens.
At Work – They call them supervisors or managers.

Picking lemons:

Sally Mulligan of Ontario decided to take one of the jobs that most Canadians are not willing to do. The woman applying for a job in a lemon grove seemed to be far too qualified. She had a liberal arts degree from the University of Toronto and had worked as a social worker and school teacher.

The foreman frowned and said, 'Have to ask you. Have you had any actual experience in picking lemons?'

To this, Sally replied, 'Well, yes, as a matter of fact, I have! I've been divorced three times, owned two Dodges, voted for the Liberals and the NDP and cheer for the Toronto Maple Leafs!

Stupid questions:

Those who say, 'There is no such thing as a stupid question' have never worked in Customer Service.

Vacuum cleaner salesman:

Myra Rhodes, an elderly lady, answered a knock on the door one day, to be confronted by a well-dressed young man carrying a vacuum cleaner.

'Good morning, Ma'am,' said the young man. 'If I could take a couple minutes of your time, I would like to demonstrate the very latest in high-powered vacuum cleaners.'

'Go away!' said Myra brusquely. 'I'm broke and haven't got any money,' and she proceeded to close the door.

Quick as a flash, the young man wedged his foot in the door and pushed it wide open. 'Don't be too hasty,' he commanded. 'Not until you have at least seen my demonstration.' And with that, he emptied a bucket of horse manure onto her hallway carpet.

'Now, if this vacuum cleaner does not remove all traces of this horse manure from your carpet, Madam, I will personally eat the remainder.'

Myra stepped back and said with a smile, 'Well let me get you a spoon, young man because they cut off my electricity this morning.'

I hate my job!

When you have an 'I hate my job day;' [Even if you're retired, you sometimes have those days] Try this out:

Stop at your pharmacy and go to the thermometer section and purchase a rectal thermometer made by Johnson & Johnson. Be very sure you get this brand.

When you get home, lock your doors, draw the curtains and disconnect the phone so you will not be disturbed. Change into very comfortable clothing and sit in your favourite chair. Open the package and remove the thermometer.

Now, carefully place it on a table or a surface so that it will not become chipped or broken. Now the fun part begins.

Take out the literature from the box and read it carefully. You will notice that in small print there is this statement: 'Every Rectal Thermometer made by Johnson & Johnson is personally tested and then sanitized.'

Now, close your eyes and repeat out loud five times,' I am so glad I do not work in the thermometer quality control department at Johnson & Johnson!'

Have a nice day; and remember, there is always someone else with a job that is more of a pain in the butt than yours!

CHAPTER 13

IS THAT RIGHT?

Deck of cards:

Each king in a deck of playing cards represents a great king from history.

Spades: King David
Clubs: Alexander the Great
Hearts: Charlemagne
Diamonds: Julius Caesar

Athletic Festival:

A slave girl from Sardinia named Gedophamee was attending a great but as yet unnamed athletic festival 2,500 years ago in Greece. In those days, the athletes performed naked. To prevent unwanted arousal while competing, the men imbibed freely on a drink containing saltpetre before and throughout the variety of events.

At the opening ceremonial parade, Gedophamee observed the first wave of naked magnificent males marching towards her and exclaimed: 'Oh! Limp pricks!'

Over the next two and a half millenniums that morphed into the 'Olympics.'

This N That:

- The trouble with life is that you're half way through it before you realize that it's one of those 'do it yourself' affairs.
- Technically, if you don't cut a cake and just eat the whole thing with a fork, you still only had one piece of cake!
- Don't let your worries get the best of you. Remember, Moses started out as a basket case.

- Have you ever looked at someone and knew that the wheel was turning, but the hamster was dead?
- Why does toilet paper need a commercial – who isn't buying it?
- Common sense is a flower that doesn't grow in everyone's garden.
- Everything is changing. People are taking their comedians seriously and the politicians as a joke.
- I don't like making plans for the day because then the word 'premeditated' gets thrown around in the court room.
- An old Irish farmer's dog goes missing and the farmer is inconsolable.
  His wife says 'Why don't you put an advert in the paper?'
  He does, but two weeks later the dog is still missing.
  'What did you put in the paper?' his wife asks.
  'Here boy,' he replies.
- Some things are better left unsaid which I generally realize right after I've said them.
- I was walking down the footpath and slipped in dog poo. A minute later, another man did exactly the same thing. I said, 'I just did that,' so he punched me and said to use a toilet next time.
- Time flies like an arrow, fruit flies like a banana.
- 'I stand corrected' said the man in orthopaedic shoes.
- I told the doctor that I broke my arm in two places; he told me to stop going to those places.
- If you really want to do something, you'll find a way. If you don't – you'll find an excuse.
- Home – where I can look ugly and enjoy it.
- Why I don't have any tattoos – for the same reason you don't put a bumper sticker on a Ferrari.
- Nights in England are coal black, making parachute jumps difficult and dangerous. So we attach small lights called chemlites to our jumpsuits to make ourselves

visible to the rest of our team. Late one night, lost after a practice jump, we knocked on the door of a small cottage. When a woman answered, she was greeted by the sight of five men festooned in glowing chemlites. 'Excuse me,' I said. 'Can you tell me where we are?'
In a thick English accent, the woman replied, 'Earth.'

- Sometimes you have to burn a few bridges to stop the crazies from following you.
- Why is it that the one who snores the loudest is always the first to fall asleep?
- Calories are the little bastards that get together at night in my closet and sew my clothes tighter. My closet is infested with the little shits.
- Say what you want about the South, but no one retires and moves up north [except in Australia that is.]
- The economy is so bad, if the bank returns your cheque marked 'insufficient funds,' you call and ask if they meant you or them.
- Robbing Peter to pay Paul means that Peter gets screwed.
- Guard at Government House, 'We've increased security at parliament house to protect your way of life.'
  Grumpy old man, 'Good. Keeping those bastards locked up is a great idea.'
- Sometimes I sit quietly and wonder why I'm not in a mental asylum… then I take a look around and realize that maybe I already am!
- I have so many problems that if a new one comes along today, it will be at least two weeks before I can worry about it.
- Contentment is not the fulfilment of what you want, but the realisation of how much you already have.
- It's not what happens to you in life that matters, it's how you handle what happens to you that really matters.

- At one time we would hang anyone who plotted to kill us in our own country. Now we give them benefits and housing.
- Every day, thousands of innocent plants are killed by vegetarians. Help end the violence – eat bacon.
- I hate it when the voices in my head go silent. I never know what they're planning.
- What happens if a politician drowns in a river? This is pollution. What happens if all of them drown? That's a solution.
- If people could read my mind - I'd get slapped in the face a lot.
- Two Irishmen find a mirror on the road. The first one picks it up and says, 'Blow me down. I know this face, but I can't put a name to it.'
The second man picks it up and exclaims, 'You daft bugger - it's me.'
- A visiting foreigner has been shot in the head with a starting piston; police say it's definitely race related.
- I'm not lazy; I just really enjoy doing nothing.
- After 100 years lying on the sea bed, Irish divers were amazed to find that the Titanic's swimming pool was still full.
- The Irish have solved their own fuel problems. They have imported fifty million tons of sand from Iran and they're going to drill for their own oil.
- Where do you learn how to make banana splits?
In Sunday school.
- What kind of underwear do reporters wear?
News briefs.
- What did one wall say to the other?
I'll meet you at the corner.
- Why did the strawberry call the emergency services number?
It was in a jam.
- What did Tennessee?

The same thing Arkansas.
- Why didn't the girl take the bus home?
Because her mom would make her take it back.
- Why was the baseball game so hot?
Because all the fans left.
- What do you call a story about a broken pencil?
Pointless.
- How do you fix a broken vegetable?
With tomato paste.
- Why did the class clown take a computer to school?
Her mom told her to bring an apple for the teacher.
- Where are cars most likely to get flat tires?
At forks in the road.
- How do they serve smart hamburgers?
On honour rolls.
- What is the world's longest punctuation mark?
The hundred-yard dash.
- Why did the calendar write its will?
Its days were numbered.
- In what school do you learn how to greet people?
Hi school.
- What school do you have to drop out of to graduate from it?
Parachute school.
- Where does Friday come before Monday?
In the dictionary.
- Why was six scared of seven?
Because seven 'ate' nine.
- Why does Humpty Dumpty love autumn?
Because Humpty Dumpty had a great fall.
- How do you make a tissue dance?
Put a little booger in it.
- It's better to walk alone than with a crowd going in the wrong direction.
- You cannot hang out with negative people and expect to live a positive life.

- One of the hardest decisions you'll ever face in life is choosing whether to walk away or try harder.
- Music is what feelings sound like.
- The mind replays what the heart can't delete.
- A pretty face is nothing if you have an ugly heart.
- Some people are old at 18 and some are young at 90 – time is a concept that humans created.
- When nothing goes right – go left.
- The YKK on your zipper stands for Yoshida Kogyo Kabushikigaisha, a Japanese company that is the world's largest manufacturer of zippers.
- Camping – where you spend a small fortune to live like a homeless person.
- I want to grow my own food, but can't find bacon seeds.
- I'm starting meetings at my home for people who have OCD (Obsessive Compulsive Disorder). I don't have it myself. I'm just hoping they'll take a look at the mess and start cleaning.
- There are more stars in space than there are grains of sand on every beach on Earth.
- A Blue Whales heart is so big, that a small child can swim through the veins.
- There's enough water in Lake Superior to cover all of North and South America in one foot of water.
- If you dug a hole to the centre of the Earth and dropped a book down, it would take 45 minutes to reach the bottom.
- The Great Pyramid was built in 2560 BC.
- Cleopatra lived from 69 BC – 30 BC (only 39 years).
- In 1903 the Wright Brothers flew for the first time. Sixty-six years later, in 1969 man landed on the moon.
- Be careful when following the masses – sometimes the 'm' is silent.
- When you're dead, you don't know you're dead – it's only difficult for others. It's the same when you're stupid.

- I never argue – I just explain why I'm right.
- I prefer not to think before speaking. I like being just as surprised as everyone else by what comes out of my mouth.
- Have you ever listened to someone for a while and wondered who ties their shoelaces for them?
- So when is this 'old enough to know better' supposed to kick in?
- I'm only responsible for what I say; not for what you understand.
- My people skills are just fine. It's my tolerance to idiots that needs work.
- You know that little thing inside your head that keeps you from saying things you shouldn't? Unfortunately, I don't have one of those.
- The fact that there's a highway to Hell and only a stairway to Heaven says a lot about anticipated traffic numbers.
- I speak my mind because it hurts to bite my tongue all the time.
- Don't confuse my personality with my attitude. My personality is who I am – my attitude depends on who you are.
- Calm down, take a deep breath and hold it for about 20 minutes.
- If you ate a polar bear's liver, you would die of a vitamin A overdose.
- Lego makes more tires than any other company in the world including actual tire companies.
- All the American flags on the moon have been bleached white by radiation from the sun.
- There are 18.6 million vacant homes in the United States. That's enough for every six homeless people in America to have a home.
- The combined weight of all ants on Earth is about the same as the combined weight of all humans.

- Putting dry tea bags in smelly shoes will absorb the odour.
- Alexander the Great conquered half the known world by the age of 22.
- Breathing in Mumbai for one day is equivalent to smoking two and a half packages of cigarettes.
- Because it takes so long for their light to reach Earth, many of the stars you see at night are long gone.
- In 2010, workers at Ground Zero found an 18th century wooden ship underneath the World Trade Centre rubble.
- Before there were clocks, there were candle clocks that burned a set number of hours. If you wanted a reminder or alarm, you would push a nail at the desired time on the candle and when it melted to that point, the nail would fall and clank on the metal candle holder.
- There are 1,000 seconds in 16 minutes
  1,000,000 seconds in 11 days and
  One billion seconds in 32 years. Use every one of them.
- Here's one to cheer you up: 'I wish I was a Glow-worm. A Glow-worm's never glum 'cos how can you be grumpy, when the sun shines from your bum?'

Aussie Burgers:

Sign in Australian restaurant: Aussie Burger – the way they were before McDonald's stuffed 'em up.

An old snake goes to see his doctor:

'Doc, I need something for my eyes – can't see well these days.'

The Doc fixes him up with a pair of glasses and tells him to return in two weeks. The snake comes back in two weeks and tells the doctor he's very depressed.

Doc says, 'What's the problem – didn't the glasses help you?'

'The glasses are fine doc, I just discovered I've been living with a garden hose the past two years!'

Some truisms:

- Women spend more time wondering what men are thinking than men spend thinking.
- Give me ambiguity or give me something else.
- He who laughs last thinks slowest.
- Is it wrong that only one company makes the game Monopoly?
- Women sometimes make fools of men, but most guys are the do-it-yourself type.
- I was going to give him a nasty look, but he already had one.
- Change is inevitable, except from a vending machine.
- The grass may be greener on the other side but at least you don't have to mow it.
- I like long walks, especially when they're taken by people who annoy me.
- I was going to wear my camouflage shirt today, but I couldn't find it.
- If at first you don't succeed, skydiving is not for you.
- Sometimes I wake up grumpy; other times I let her sleep.
- Money is the root of all wealth.
- No matter how much you push the envelope, it'll still be stationery.
- Some day everything will make perfect sense. But for now, laugh at the confusion, smile through the tears and keep reminding yourself that everything happens for a reason.
- You never appreciate what you have until it's gone – toilet paper is a good example.
- Your value doesn't decrease based on someone else's inability to see your worth.

Steven Wright's humour:

If you're not familiar with the work of Steven Wright, he's the famous erudite scientist who once said: 'I woke up one morning, and all of my stuff had been stolen and replaced by exact duplicates.'

His mind sees things differently than most of us do. Here are some of his gems:

1 - I'd kill for a Nobel Peace Prize.
2 - Borrow money from pessimists - they don't expect it back.
3 - Half the people you know are below average.
4 - 99% of lawyers give the rest a bad name.
5 - 82.7% of all statistics are made up on the spot.
6 - A conscience is what hurts when all your other parts feel so good.
7 - A clear conscience is usually the sign of a bad memory
8 - If you want the rainbow, you've got to put up with the rain.
9 - All those who believe in psycho kinesis, raise my hand.
10 - The early bird may get the worm, but the second mouse gets the cheese.
11 - I almost had a psychic girlfriend... But she left me before we met.
12 - Okay, so what's the speed of dark?
13 - How do you tell when you're out of invisible ink?
14 - If everything seems to be going well, you have obviously overlooked something.
15 - Depression is merely anger without enthusiasm.
16 - When everything is coming your way, you're in the wrong lane.
17 - Ambition is a poor excuse for not having enough sense to be lazy.
18 - Hard work pays off in the future; laziness pays off now.
19 - I intend to live forever... So far, so good.
20 - If Barbie is so popular, why do you have to buy her friends?
21 - Eagles may soar, but weasels don't get sucked into jet engines.

22 - What happens if you get scared half to death twice?
23 - My mechanic told me, 'I couldn't repair your brakes, so I made your horn louder.'
24 - Why do psychics have to ask you for your name?
25 - If at first you don't succeed, destroy all evidence that you tried.
26 - A conclusion is the place where you got tired of thinking.
27 - Experience is something you don't get until just after you need it.
28 - The hardness of the butter is proportional to the softness of the bread.
29 - To steal ideas from one person is plagiarism; to steal from many is research.
30 - The problem with the gene pool is that there is no lifeguard.
31 - The sooner you fall behind; the more time you'll have to catch up.
32 - The colder the x-ray table, the more of your body is required to be on it.
33 - Everyone has a photographic memory; some just don't have film.

And an all-time favourite:

34 - If your car could travel at the speed of light, would your headlights work?

Landscape sign:

Spring is here. I'm so excited, I wet my plants.

Supermarket sign:

Looking for hot chicks? Go to the deli.

Sign in front of home:

Divorce yard sale – hurry before spouse comes home.

The Motorbike:

Q: Why did the Maori cross the road on a motorbike?

A: To get to the other side.

Q: Why did the pakeha (white Kiwi) cross the road?
A: To get his motorbike back!

Restaurant sign:

Today's special: Buy one fish and chips for the price of two and receive a second fish and chips absolutely free.

Canadian vs Australian English:

Canadian	Australian
candy	lollies
cookies	bickies
wallet	purse
purse	handbag
sofa	lounge
asphalt	bitumen
tires	tyres
pants	trousers
receipt	docket
flashlight	torch
toque	beanie
sunglasses	sunnies
afternoon	arvo
truck	ute
university	uni
pregnant	preggie
baby	bub
mom	mum
sweater	jumper

Did you know:

- Until the 1850's, there were no right and left shoes — they were identical.
- Scientists say that your left ear is better at hearing music, the right is better for conversations.
- Coca Cola only sold 25 bottles the first year, but kept on going. Never give up!

- A large portion of the Oxford English dictionary was written by a murderer from a mental institute.
- A jiffy is an actual unit of time. 1 jiffy = 1/100 of a second.

The new reality:

It seems that lately my life has been getting more complicated, and I want to thank those of you who are brave enough to still associate with me regardless of what I have become. The following is a recap of my current identity:

- I was born white, which makes me a racist.
- I am a fiscal and moral conservative, which makes me a fascist.
- I am heterosexual, which makes me a homophobe.
- I am non-union, which makes me a traitor to the working class and an ally of big business.
- I am a Christian, which makes me an infidel.
- I am older than 65 and retired, which makes me a useless old person.
- I think and I reason; therefore, I doubt much that the main stream media tells me, which makes me a reactionary.
- I am proud of my heritage and our inclusive American culture, which makes me a xenophobe.
- I value my safety and that of my family; therefore, I appreciate the police and the legal system, which makes me a right-wing extremist.
- I believe in hard work, fair play, and fair compensation according to each individual's merits, which makes me anti-social.
- I, and my friends, acquired a good education without student loans and no debt at completion, which makes me some kind of odd underachiever.
- I believe in the defence and protection of America by all citizens, which makes me a militarist.

- Please help me come to terms with this, because I 'm not sure who I am anymore!
- Newest problem... In USA, I'm not sure which bathroom I should use.

The Confused One!

The first line:

For all lovers of good writing, here are this year's winners of the Bulwer-Lytton contest, (a.k.a. 'It Was a dark and Stormy Night' contest) run by the English Department of San Jose State University, wherein one writes only the first line of a bad novel.

10. As a scientist, Throckmorton knew that if he were ever to break wind in the echo chamber, he would never hear the end of it.

9. Just beyond the Narrows, the river widens.

8. With a curvaceous figure that Venus would have envied, a tanned unblemished oval face framed with lustrous thick brown hair, deep azure-blue eyes fringed with long black lashes, perfect teeth that vied for competition, and a small straight nose, Marilee had a beauty that defied description.

7. Andre, a simple peasant, had only one thing on his mind as he crept along the East wall: "Andre creep – Andre creep – Andre creep."

6. Stanislaus Smedley, a man always on the cutting edge of narcissism, was about to give his body and soul to a back alley sex-change surgeon to become the woman he loved.

5. Although Sarah had an abnormal fear of mice, it did not keep her from eking out a living at a local pet store.

4. Stanley looked quite bored and somewhat detached, but then penguins often do.

3. Like an over-ripe beefsteak tomato rimmed with cottage cheese, the corpulent remains of Santa Claus lay dead on the hotel floor.

2. Mike Hardware was the kind of private eye who didn't know the meaning of the word "fear;" a man who could laugh in the face of danger and spit in the eye of death – in short, a moron with suicidal tendencies.

1. The sun oozed over the horizon, shoved aside darkness, crept along the greensward, and, with sickly fingers, pushed through the castle window, revealing the pillaged princess, hand at throat, crown asunder, gasping in frenzied horror at the sated, sodden amphibian lying beside her, disbelieving the magnitude of the frog's deception, screaming madly, 'You lied!'

Cake and eat it too:

A member of a diet club bemoaned her lack of will-power. She had made her family's favourite cake over the weekend, she explained, and they had eaten half of it. The next day, however, the uneaten half beckoned. She cut herself a slice. Then another, and another. By the time she had polished off the cake, she knew her husband would be disappointed.

'What did he say when he found out?' one club member asked.

'He never found out,' she said. 'I made another cake and ate half.'

When I was a boy:

When I was a boy, my Momma would send me down to a corner store with $1 and I'd come back with five bags of potatoes, two loaves of bread, three bottles of milk, a hunk of cheese, a box of tea and six eggs.

You can't do that now... too many security cameras.

Wrong response:

An Emergency call taker in London Ambulance Control has been dismissed from her job, much to the dismay of colleagues who are reportedly unhappy with her treatment.

It seems a male caller dialled 999 from a mobile phone stating, 'I am depressed and lying here on a railway track - I am waiting for the train to come so I can finally meet Allah.'

Apparently 'Remain calm and stay on the line,' was not considered to be an appropriate or correct response.

Service:

We offer three kinds of service: Good, Cheap and Fast – you can pick any two:

- Good service cheap – won't be fast.
- Good service fast – won't be cheap.
- Fast service cheap – won't be good.

Sleep:

You know that awesome feeling when you get into bed, fall right asleep, stay asleep all night and wake up feeling refreshed and ready to take on the day? Nope – I don't either.

Bad dog:

The police came to my home earlier and said that my dog had chased someone on a bike. I said, 'You must be joking officer – my dog doesn't have a bike.

Chinese Quote:

Some people, no matter how old they get, never lose their beauty. They merely move it from their face to their heart.

CHAPTER 14

MISCELLANEOUS

English weather:

In deference to the Archbishop of Canterbury and the Royal Commission for Political Correctness, it was announced today that the local climate in the UK should no longer be referred to as 'English weather.' Rather than offend a sizeable portion of the population it will now be referred to as 'Muslim Weather.' In other words – 'partly Sunni, but mostly Shi'ite.'

Letter to Iarnród Éireann: (the Irish Railway Company)

Gentlemen,
I have been riding your trains daily for the last two years, and the service on your line seems to be getting worse every day. I am tired of standing in the aisle all the time on a 14-mile trip. I think the transportation system is worse than that enjoyed by people 2,000 years ago.
Yours truly,
Patrick Finnegan

Dear Mr. Finnegan,
We received your letter with reference to the shortcomings of our service and believe you are somewhat confused in your history. The only mode of transportation 2,000 years ago was by foot.
Sincerely,
Iarnród Éireann

Gentlemen,
I am in receipt of your letter, and I think you are the ones who are confused in your history. If you will refer to the Bible and the Book of David, 9th Chapter, you will find that

Balaam rode to town on his ass. That, Gentlemen, is something I have not been able to do on your train in the last two years!

Yours truly,

Patrick Finnegan

Psychology class:

It was a practical session in the psychology class. The professor showed a large cage with a male rat in it. The rat was in the middle of the cage. The professor kept a piece of cake on one side and a female rat on the other side. The male rat ran towards the cake and ate it.

Then, the professor changed the cake and replaced it with some bread. The male rat ran towards the bread. This experiment went on with the professor changing the food every time. And, every time, the male rat ran towards the food item and never towards the female rat.

The professor said, 'This experiment shows that food is the greatest strength and attraction.

Then, one of the students from the back rows said, 'Sir, why don't you change the female rat. She may be his wife!'

The Scottish cow:

The only cow in a small town in Ireland stopped giving milk. Then the town folk found they could buy a cow in Scotland quite cheaply. So, they brought the cow over from Scotland.

It was absolutely wonderful. It produced lots of milk every day and everyone was happy.

They bought a bull to mate with the cow to get more cows, so they'd never have to worry about their milk supply again. They put the bull in the pasture with the cow but whenever the bull tried to mount the cow, the cow would move away.

No matter what approach the bull tried, the cow would move away from the bull, and he was never able to do the deed.

The people were very upset and decided to go to the Vet, who was very wise, tell him what was happening and ask his advice.

'Whenever the bull tries to mount our cow, she moves away. If he approaches from the back, she moves forward. When he approaches her from the front, she backs off. If he attempts it from the one side, she walks away to the other side.'

The Vet rubbed his chin thoughtfully and pondered this before asking 'Did you by chance, buy this cow in Scotland?'

The people were dumbfounded, since no one had ever mentioned that they had brought the cow over from Scotland.

'You are truly a wise Vet,' they said.

'How did you know we got the cow from Scotland?'

The Vet replied with a distant look in his eye: 'My wife is from Scotland.'

Mothers:

If a mother asks you a question, it's better to tell the truth because chances are she's asking because she already knows the answer.

Fun with Ronnie Barker:

Sounds better when you read this aloud! This was originally shown on BBC TV back in the seventies. Ronnie Barker could say all of this without a snigger. The irony is that they received not one complaint. The speed of delivery must have been too much for the whining herds. Try getting through it without converting the spoonerisms [and not wetting your pants] as you read.

This is the story of Rindercella and her sugly isters.

Rindercella and her sugly isters lived in a marge lansion. Rindercella worked very hard frubbing sloors, emptying poss pits, and shivelling shot. At the end of the day, she was knucking fackered. The sugly isters were right bugly astards. One was called Mary Hinge, and the other was called Betty Swallocks; they were really forrible huckers; they had fetty sweet and fatty swannies. The sugly isters had tickets to go to the ball, but the cotton runts would not let Rindercella go.

Suddenly there was a bucking fang, and her gairy fodmother appeared. Her name was Shairy Hithole and she was a light rucking fesbian. She turned a pumpkin and six mite wice into a hucking cuge farriage with six dandy ronkeys who had buge hollocks and dig bicks. The gairy fodmother told Rindercella to be back by dimnlight otherwise, there would be a cucking falamity. At the ball, Rindercella was dancing with the prandsome hince when suddenly the clock struck twelve. 'Mist all chucking frighty!' said Rindercella, and she ran out tripping barse over ollocks, so dropping her slass glipper.

The very next day the prandsome hince knocked on Rindercella's door and the sugly isters let him in. Suddenly, Betty Swallocks lifted her leg and let off a fig bart. 'Who's fust jarted?' asked the prandsome hince. 'Blame that fugly ucker over there!' said Mary Hinge. When the stinking brown cloud had lifted, he tried the slass glipper on both the sugly isters without success and their feet stucking funk. Betty Swallocks was ducking fisgusted and gave the prandsome hince a knack in the kickers. This was not difficult as he had bucking fuge halls and a hig bard on. He tried the slass glipper on Rindercella and it fitted pucking ferfectly.

Rindercella and the prandsome hince were married. The pransome hince lived his life in lucking fuxury, and Rindercella lived hers with a follen swanny!

Bear on roof:

A man in Michigan's Upper Peninsula wakes up one morning to find a bear on his roof. So he looks in the yellow pages and, sure enough, there's an ad for 'Up North Bear Removers.'

He calls the number and the bear remover says he'll be over in 30 minutes.

The bear remover arrives and gets out of his van. He's got a ladder, a baseball bat, a 12-gauge shotgun and a mean, heavily scarred, old pit bull.

'What are you going to do?' the homeowner asks.

'I'm going to put this ladder up against the roof, then I'm going up there and knock the bear off the roof with this baseball bat. When the bear falls off the roof, the pit bull is trained to grab his testicles and not let go. The bear will then be subdued enough for me to put him in the cage in the back of the van.'

He then hands the shotgun to the homeowner

'What's the shotgun for?' asks the homeowner.

'If the bear knocks me off the roof, shoot the dog.'

Distinctive signs:

- Jamaican Me Hungry - Caribbean Cuisine
- Hairy Pop-ins – Pet nannies
- Carl's Pane in the Glass
- A salt & Battery - Fish and Chips
- Shear Heaven – Hair design
- Sew What? - Alterations & Tailoring
- Eggs Eggetera - Store name
- Bags Bunny – Handbag shop

- Lettus Eat - Sandwich bar
- Nin Com Soup – Chinese restaurant
- Cycloanalysts – Bicycle shop
- Optimeyes – Opticians
- Spruce Springclean – Upholstery cleaning
- Sure Lock Loans
- Bits & PCs – Computer store
- Sofa So Good – Furniture sales
- Frock Off – Women's fashions
- Lord of the Fries – Fish & Chips
- Woofs A Daisy – Pet supplies
- Spex City - Opticians
- Plaice Station – Restaurant
- Thai me up – Thai restaurant
- Get Laid Professionally – Carpet layers
- Thistle Do Nicely – Clothing shop
- The Codfather – Quality fish & Chips
- Barber Blacksheep - Barber
- Jack the Stripper – Wood stripping
- Back to the Fuchsia – Flower shop
- Florest Gump – Flower Shop
- A sign in a shoe repair store in Vancouver read: We will heel you. We will save your sole. We will even dye for you.
- In a Podiatrist's office: Time wounds all heels.
- At an Optometrist's Office: If you don't see what you're looking for, you've come to the right place.
- On a Plumber's truck: We repair what your husband fixed.
- On another Plumber's truck: Don't sleep with a drip. Call your plumber.
- At a Tire Shop in Milwaukee: Invite us to your next blowout.
- On an Electrician's truck: Let us remove your shorts.

- In a Non-smoking Area: If we see smoke, we will assume you are on fire and will take appropriate action.
- At a Car Dealership: The best way to get back on your feet - miss a car payment.
- Outside a Muffler Shop: No appointment necessary. We hear you coming.
- In a Veterinarian's waiting room: Be back in five minutes. Sit! Stay!
- At the Electric Company: We would be delighted if you send in your payment on time. However, if you don't, YOU will be de-lighted.
- In a Restaurant window: Don't stand there and be hungry; come on in and get fed up.
- In the front yard of a Funeral Home: Drive carefully. We'll wait.
- At a Propane Filling Station: Thank Heaven for little grills.
- In a Chicago Radiator Shop: Best place in town to take a leak.
- Toilet sign: Men – to the left because women are always right.

And the best one for last.

- Sign on the back of a Septic Tank Truck: Caution - This Truck is full of Political Promises.

Bagpiper at funeral:

Time is like a river. You cannot touch the water twice, because the flow that has passed will never pass again. Enjoy every moment of life.

As a bagpiper, I play many gigs. Recently I was asked by a funeral director to play at a graveside service for a homeless man. He had no family or friends, so the service was to be at a pauper's cemetery in the Nova Scotia back country. As I was not familiar with the backwoods, I became lost and being a typical man, I didn't stop for directions.

I finally arrived an hour late and saw the funeral guy had evidently gone and the hearse was nowhere in sight. Only the diggers and crew were still there and they were eating lunch. I felt badly and apologised to the men for being late. I went to the side of the grave and looked down and the vault lid was already in place.

I didn't know what else to do, so I started to play. The workers put down their lunches and began to gather around. I played out my heart and soul for this man with no family and friends. I played like I've never played before for this homeless man and as I played 'Amazing Grace,' the workers began to weep. They wept, I wept, we all wept together. When I finished, I packed up my bagpipes and started for my car.

Though my head was hung low, my heart was full. As I opened the door to my car, I heard one of the workers say, 'I never seen anything like that before and I've been putting in septic tanks for twenty years.'

A Scotsman's first baseball game:

A Scotsman moves to North America and attends his first baseball game. The first batter approaches the batters' box, takes a few swings, then hits a double. Everyone is on their feet screaming 'Run!'

The next batter hits a single. The Scotsman listens as the crowd again cheers 'Run!'

The Scotsman is enjoying the game and begins screaming with the fans. The fifth batter comes up and four balls go by, and the umpire calls: 'Walk.'

The batter starts his slow trot to first base. The Scot stands up and screams, 'Run ye lazy bastard, run!'

The people around him begin laughing. Embarrassed, the Scot sits back down.

A friendly fan notes the man's embarrassment, leans over and explains, 'He can't run - he has four balls.'

The Scot stands up and screams: 'Walk with pride, Laddie!'

Golf accident:

Many years ago, I accidentally overturned my golf cart. Elizabeth, a very attractive and keen golfer, who lived in a villa on the golf course, heard the noise and called out: 'Are you okay, what's your name?'

'It's John, and I'm okay thanks,' I replied as I pulled myself out of the twisted cart.

'John,' she said, (firm loose breasts undulating beneath her white silky robe) 'forget your troubles. Come to my villa, rest a while and I'll help you get the cart up later.'

'That's mighty nice of you,' I answered, 'but I don't think my wife would like it.'

'Oh, come on now' Elizabeth insisted.

She was so very pretty, very, very sexy and very persuasive ... I was weak.

'Well okay,' I finally agreed but thought to myself, 'my wife won't like it.'

After a couple of restorative Scotch and waters, I thanked Elizabeth. 'I feel a lot better now, but I know my wife is going to be really upset. So I'd best go now.'

'Don't be silly!' Elizabeth said with a smile, letting her robe fall open slightly. 'She won't know anything. By the way, where is she?'

'Still under the cart I guess,' he replied sheepishly.

Golf Goodies:

- I was one under today
    - One under a tree
    - One under a bush

- One under the water
- They call it golf because all other 4-letter words were taken.
- The school teacher was taking her first golf lesion.
  'Is the word spelled p-u-t or p-u-t-t?' she asked the instructor.
  'P-u-t-t is correct.' He replied. 'Put means placing a thing where you want it. Putt means merely a vain attempt to do the same thing.'
- Golf is the art of playing fetch with yourself.
- Golfer, 'Do you think I can get there with a 5 iron?'
  Caddy, 'Eventually sir.'

The history of the middle finger:

Well, now... here's something I never knew before, and now that I know it, I feel compelled to send it on to my more intelligent friends in the hope that they, too, will feel edified.

Before the Battle of Agincourt in 1415, the French, anticipating victory over the English, proposed to cut off the middle finger of all captured English soldiers. Without the middle finger it would be impossible to draw the renowned English longbow and therefore they would be incapable of fighting in the future. This famous English longbow was made of the native English Yew tree, and the act of drawing the longbow was known as 'plucking the yew' (or 'pluck yew').

Much to the bewilderment of the French, the English won a major upset and they began mocking the French by waving their middle fingers at the defeated French, saying, See, we can still pluck yew! Since 'pluck yew' is rather difficult to say, the difficult consonant cluster at the beginning has gradually changed to a labiodentals fricative F', and thus the words often used in conjunction with the one-finger-salute! It is also because of the pheasant feathers on the arrows used with the longbow that the symbolic gesture is known as 'giving the bird.'

And you thought you knew every plucking thing.

The New Zealander:

A person of colour and a New Zealander go into a pastry shop in north Cairns.

The black guy whisks three cookies into his pocket with lightning speed. The baker doesn't notice.

The black guy says to the New Zealander, 'You see how clever we are? You New Zealanders can never beat that!'

The New Zealander says to the black guy, 'Watch this. Any New Zealander is smarter than you, and I'll prove it to you.'

He says to the baker, 'Give me a cookie and I'll show you a great magic trick!'

The baker gives him the cookie, that the New Zealander promptly eats.

Then he says to the baker, 'I need another cookie to show you this magic trick.'

The baker is getting suspicious, but he gives it to him. He eats this one too.

Then he says again, "Give me one more cookie...' The baker is getting angry now, but gives him one anyway. The New Zealander eats this one too.

Now the baker is really mad, and he yells, 'Okay... but where's your famous magic trick?'

The New Zealander says...'Look in the black guy's pocket!'

Ten little pigs:

A farmer had five female pigs. Times were hard, so he decided to take them to the county fair and sell them. At the fair, he met another farmer who owned five male pigs. After talking a bit, they decided to mate the pigs and split everything 50/50.

The farmers lived 60 miles apart, so they decided to drive 30 miles each and find a field in which to let the pigs mate. The first morning, the farmer with the female pigs got up at 5 am, loaded the pigs into the family station wagon, (which was the only vehicle he had) and drove the thirty miles.

While the pigs were mating, he asked the other farmer, 'How will I know if they are pregnant?'

The other farmer replied, 'If they're lying in the grass tomorrow morning, they're pregnant. If they're lying in the mud, they're not.'

The next morning the pigs were rolling in the mud, so he hosed them off, loaded them into the family station wagon again and proceeded to try again.

This continued each morning for more than a week and both farmers were worn out. The next morning, he was too tired to get out of bed. He called his wife, 'Honey, please look outside and tell me whether the pigs are in the mud or in the grass.'

'Neither,' yelled his wife, 'they're in the station wagon. And one of them is honking the horn.'

New version of the three bears:

Baby bear goes downstairs, sits in his small chair at the table. He looks into his small bowl. It is empty. 'Who's been eating my porridge?' he squeaks.

Daddy Bear arrives at the big table and sits in his big chair. He looks into his big bowl and it's also empty. 'Who's been eating my porridge?' he roars.

Mommy Bear puts her head through the serving hatch from the kitchen and yells, 'For God's sake, how many times do I have to go through this with you idiots?

It was Mommy Bear who got up first.

It was Mommy Bear who woke everyone in the house.

It was Mommy Bear who made the coffee.

It was Mommy Bear who unloaded the dishwasher from last night and put everything away.

It was Mommy Bear who swept the floor in the kitchen.

It was Mommy Bear who went out in the cold early morning air to fetch the newspaper and croissants.

It was Mommy Bear who set the damn table.

'It was Mommy Bear who walked the bloody dog, cleaned the cat's litter tray, gave them their food, and refilled their water.

And now that you've decided to drag your sorry bear-arses downstairs and grace Mommy Bear with your grumpy presence, listen carefully, because I'm only going to say this once... 'I haven't made the f****** porridge yet!'

Lexophiles:

- A man's home is his castle, in a manor of speaking.
- Dijon vu - the same mustard as before.
- Practice safe eating - always use condiments.
- Shotgun wedding - A case of wife or death.
- A man needs a mistress just to break the monogamy.
- A hangover is the wrath of grapes.
- Does the name Pavlov ring a bell?
- Condoms should be used on every conceivable occasion.
- Reading while sunbathing makes you well red.
- When two egotists meet, it's an I for an I.
- A bicycle can't stand on its own because it is two tired.
- What's the definition of a will? It's a dead give-away.
- In democracy your vote counts. In feudalism your count votes.
- She was engaged to a boy with a wooden leg but broke it off.

- A chicken crossing the road is poultry in motion.
- The man who fell into an upholstery machine is fully recovered.
- You feel stuck with your debt if you can't budge it.
- Local Area Network in Australia - the LAN down under.
- Every calendar's days are numbered.
- A lot of money is tainted - Taint yours and taint mine.
- A boiled egg in the morning is hard to beat.
- He had a photographic memory that was never developed.
- A midget fortune-teller who escapes from prison is a small medium at large.
- Once you've seen one shopping centre, you've seen a mall.
- Bakers trade bread recipes on a knead-to-know basis.

Financial Planning explained by an Irishman in the Outback

Paddy bought a camel from a farmer for $100. The farmer agreed to deliver the camel the next day.
In the morning he drove up and said, 'Sorry son, but I have some bad news. The camel's died.'
Paddy replied, 'Well just give me my money back then.'
The farmer said, 'Can't do that. I've already spent it.'
Paddy said, "Okay then, just bring me the dead camel.'
The farmer asked, 'What are you going to do with him?'
Paddy said, 'I'm going to raffle him off.'
The farmer said, 'You can't raffle a dead camel!'
Paddy said, 'Sure I can. Watch me. I just won't tell anybody he's dead.'
A month later, the farmer met up with Paddy and asked, 'What happened with that dead camel?'
Paddy said, 'I raffled him off. I sold 500 tickets at $2 each and made a profit of $898.'
The farmer said, 'Didn't anyone complain?'
Paddy said, 'Just the guy who won. So I gave him his $2 back.'

CHAPTER 15

HISTORY

Description of the English:

One of the English national daily newspapers asked readers – What does it mean to be English.

Some of the e-mails were hilarious but this one from a chap in Switzerland stood out. 'Being English is about driving a German car to an Irish pub for a Belgian beer, and then travelling home, grabbing an Indian curry or a Turkish kebab on the way, to sit on Swedish furniture and watch American or Australian shows on a Japanese or Korean TV which will soon be powered by a Chinese nuclear power station. And the most English thing of all? Suspicion of anything foreign.'

Ancient story:

Once upon a time a fellow did a big favour for the king in a land far away. The king told the fellow he'd repay him with one of his three daughters in marriage. He'd have to choose. One girl was beautiful but could hardly cook. The second one has fairly pretty and could cook a little. The third one was fairly plain looking but could really cook.

Based on that data, who did the fellow choose?

He married the king as it's just a fairy story anyhow.

Aplomb:

His Lordship was in the study at Downtown Abbey when the butler approached and coughed discreetly.

'May I ask you a question, My Lord?'

'Go ahead, Carson,' said his Lordship.

'I'm doing a crossword in The Times and I have found a word I am not too clear on.'

'What word is that?' asked his Lordship.

'Aplomb, My Lord.'

'Now that's a difficult one to explain. I would say it is self-assurance or complete composure.'

'Thank you My Lord, but I am still a little confused.'

'Let me give you an example to make it clearer. Do you remember a few months ago when the Duke and Duchess of Cambridge came to stay with us?'

'I remember the occasion very well My Lord. It gave the staff and myself much pleasure to look after them.'

'Also,' continued the Earl of Grantham, 'do you remember when Wills plucked a rose for Kate in the rose garden?'

'I was present on that occasion My Lord, ministering to their needs.'

'While plucking the rose, a thorn embedded itself in his thumb very deeply.'

'I witnessed the incident, My Lord, and saw the Duchess remove the thorn and bandage his thumb with her own dainty handkerchief.'

'That evening the prick on his thumb was so sore, Kate had to cut up his venison from our own estate, even though it was extremely tender.'

'Yes My Lord, I did see everything that transpired that evening.'

'The next morning while you were pouring coffee for Her Ladyship, Kate inquired of Wills with a loud voice, 'Darling, does your prick still throb?'

'And you, Carson did not spill one drop of coffee! That's aplomb.'

Sir Peter John Cosgrove:

Sir Peter John Cosgrove, AK, MC (born 28 July 1947) is a retired senior Australian Army officer and the 26th Governor-General of Australia. He was sworn in on 28 March 2014, and made a Knight of the Order of Australia the same day.

General Cosgrove was interviewed on TV by Leigh Sales from the ABC. Read his reply to the lady who interviewed him concerning guns and children. Regardless of how you feel about gun laws you have to love this! This is one of the best comeback lines of all time.

This is a portion of an ABC interview between a female journalist Leigh Sales and General Cosgrove who was about to sponsor a Boy Scout Troop visiting his military Headquarters.

Leigh Sales, 'So, General Cosgrove, what things are you going to teach these young boys when they visit your base?'

General Cosgrove, 'We're going to teach them climbing, canoeing, archery and shooting.'

Leigh Sales, ''Shooting! That's a bit irresponsible, isn't it?

General Cosgrove, 'I don't see why, they'll be properly supervised on the rifle range.'

Leigh Sales, 'Don't you admit that this is a terribly dangerous activity to be teaching children?'

General Cosgrove, 'I don't see how. We will be teaching them proper rifle discipline before they even touch a firearm.'

Leigh Sales, 'But you're equipping them to become violent killers.'

General Cosgrove, 'Well, Ma'am, you're equipped to be a prostitute, but you're not one, are you?'

The broadcast went silent for 46 seconds and when it returned, the interview was over.

[Author's note: I fully agree with Leigh Sales. The last thing we need in Australia is a US gun mentality!]

Australian trivia:

- The biggest property in Australia is bigger than Belgium.
- More than 85% of Australians live within 50 km of the coast.
- Gina Reinhart, Australia's richest woman earns $1 million every half hour or $598 every second.
- Each week, 70 tourists overstay their visas in Australia.
- Australia's first police force was made up of the most well-behaved convicts.
- Saudi Arabia imports camels from Australia (mostly for meat).
- Per capita, Australians spend more money on gambling than any other nation.
- Australia is home to 20% of the world's poker machines. Half of these are found in New South Wales.
- Australia is one of the only countries where we eat the animals on our coat of arms.
- If you visit one new beach in Australia every day, it would take over 27 years to see them all.
- The Great Barrier Reef is the planet's largest living structure.
- In 2005, security guards at Canberra Parliament House were banned from calling people 'mate.' It lasted one day.
- The wine cask is an Australian invention. So is the selfie.
- In 1979, debris from NASA's space station crashed in Esperance Western Australia. The town then fined NASA $400 for littering.

- Some shopping centres and restaurants play classical music to deter teenagers from loitering.

Story of a little boy:

A grandson of slaves, a boy was born in a poor neighbourhood, of New Orleans known as the 'Back of Town.' His father abandoned the family when the child was an infant. His mother became a prostitute and the boy and his sister, had to live with their grandmother.

Early in life he proved to be gifted for music, and with three other kids he sang in the streets of New Orleans.

His first gains were the coins that were thrown to them.

A Jewish family, Karnofsky, who had immigrated from Lithuania to the USA, had pity for the 7-year-old boy and brought him into their home, initially giving 'work' in the house, to feed this hungry child. There he remained and slept in this Jewish family's home where, for the first time in his life he was treated with kindness and tenderness.

When he went to bed, Mrs. Karnovsky sang him a Russian Lullaby that he would sing with her. Later, he learned to sing and play several Russian and Jewish songs. Over time, this boy became the adopted son of this family.

The Karnofskys gave him money to buy his first musical instrument; as was the custom in the Jewish families. They sincerely admired his musical talent.

Later, when he became a professional musician and composer. He used these Jewish melodies in compositions, such as St. James Infirmary and Go Down Moses.

The little black boy grew up and wrote a book about this Jewish family, who had adopted him in 1907.

In memory of this family and until the end of his life, he wore a star of David and said that in this family, he had learned 'how to live real life and determination.'

You might recognize his name. This little boy was called Louis 'Satchmo' Armstrong. Louis Armstrong proudly spoke fluent Yiddish! And I bet you did not know any of this, and 'Satchmo' is Yiddish for 'Big Cheeks.'

Adopt a Terrorist:

Too good to miss - The Canadians know how to handle complaints. Here 's an example.

A Canadian female liberal wrote a lot of letters to the Canadian government, complaining about the treatment of captive insurgents (terrorists) being held in Afghanistan National Correctional System facilities. She demanded a response to her letter. She received back the following reply:

National Defense Headquarters
M Gen George R. Pearkes Bldg., 15 NT
101 Colonel By Drive
Ottawa, ON K1A 0K2, Canada

Dear Concerned Citizen,

Thank you for your recent letter expressing your profound concern of treatment of the Taliban and Al Qaeda terrorists captured by Canadian Forces, who were subsequently transferred to the Afghanistan Government and are currently being held by Afghan officials in Afghanistan National Correctional System facilities.

Our administration takes these matters seriously and your opinions were heard loud and clear here in Ottawa. You will be pleased to learn, thanks to the concerns of citizens like yourself, we are creating a new department here at the Department of National Defense, to be called 'Liberals Accept Responsibility for Killers' program, or L.A.R.K. for short.

In accordance with the guidelines of this new program, we have decided, on a trial basis, to divert several terrorists and place them in homes of concerned citizens such as yourself, around the country, under those citizens' personal care. Your personal detainee has been selected and is scheduled for transportation under heavily armed guard to your residence in Toronto next Monday.

Ali Mohammed Ahmed bin Mahmud is your detainee, and is to be cared for pursuant to the standards you personally demanded in your letter of complaint. You will be pleased to know that we will conduct weekly inspections to ensure that your standards of care for Ahmed are commensurate with your recommendations.

Although Ahmed is a sociopath and extremely violent, we hope that your sensitivity to what you described as his 'attitudinal problem' will help him overcome those character flaws. Perhaps you are correct in describing these problems as mere cultural differences. We understand that you plan to offer counselling and home schooling, however, we strongly recommend that you hire some assistant caretakers.

Please advise any Jewish friends, neighbours or relatives about your house guest, as he might get agitated or even violent, but we are sure you can reason with him. He is also expert at making a wide variety of explosive devices from common household products, so you may wish to keep those items locked up, unless in your opinion, this might offend him. Your adopted terrorist is extremely proficient in hand-to-hand combat and can extinguish human life with such simple items as a pencil or nail clippers. We advise that you do not ask him to demonstrate these skills either in your home or wherever you choose to take him while helping him adjust to life in our country.

Ahmed will not wish to interact with you or your daughters except sexually, since he views females as a form of property, thereby having no rights, including refusal of his sexual demand. This is a particularly sensitive subject for him.

You also should know that he has shown violent tendencies around women who fail to comply with the dress code that he will recommend as more appropriate attire. I'm sure you will come to enjoy the anonymity offered by the burka over time. Just remember that it is all part of 'respecting his culture and religious beliefs' as described in your letter

You take good care of Ahmed and remember that we will try to have a counsellor available to help you over any difficulties you encounter while Ahmed is adjusting to Canadian culture.

Thanks again for your concern. We truly appreciate it when folks like you keep us informed of the proper way to do our job and care for our fellow man. Good luck and God bless you.

Cordially,

Gordon O'Connor
Minister of National Defense

Complaints to local councils in Britain:

- It's the dogs mess that I find hard to swallow.
- 50% of the walls are damp, 50% have crumbling plaster and 50% are just plain filthy.
- Will you please send a man to look at my water – it's a funny colour and not fit to drink.
- Our lavatory seat is broken in half and is now in three pieces.

Chutzpah:

Chutzpah is a Yiddish word meaning gall, brazen nerve, effrontery, sheer guts plus arrogance; it's Yiddish and, no other work and no other language can do it justice. This example is better than 1,000 words:

A little old Jewish lady sold pretzels on a street corner for 15 cents each. Every day a young man would leave his office building at lunch time and as he passed the pretzel stand, he would leave her a quarter, but never take a pretzel. This went on for more than three years.

The two of them never spoke. One day, as the young man passed the old lady's stand and left his quarter as usual, the pretzel lady spoke to him. Without blinking an eye, she said, 'They're 35 cents now.'

No that's Chutzpah.

Walking Eagle:

Donald Trump was invited to address a major gathering of the American Indian Nation two weeks ago in upstate New York. He spoke for almost an hour about his plans for increasing every Native American's present standard of living. He referred to how he had supported every Native American issue that came to the news media.

Although Mr. Trump was vague about the details of his plans, he seemed most enthusiastic and spoke eloquently about his ideas for helping his 'red sisters and brothers.'

At the conclusion of his speech, the Tribes presented him with a plaque inscribed with his new Indian name, 'Walking Eagle.' The proud Mr. Trump accepted the plaque and then departed in his motorcade to a fundraiser, waving to the crowds.

A news reporter later asked the group of chiefs how they came to select the new name they had given to Trump. They explained that 'Walking Eagle' is the name given to a bird so full of shit it can no longer fly.

Einstein:

Einstein dies and goes to heaven only to be informed that his room is not yet ready. 'I hope you will not mind waiting in a dormitory. We are very sorry, but it's the best we can do and you will have to share the room with others' he is told by Saint Peter.

Einstein says that this is no problem at all and that there is no need to make such a great fuss. So the doorman leads him to the dorm. They enter and Albert is introduced to all of the present inhabitants. 'See, here is your first room-mate. He has an IQ of 180!'

'That's wonderful!' says Albert. 'We can discuss mathematics!'

'And here is your second room-mate. His IQ is 150!'

'That's wonderful!' says Albert. 'We can discuss physics!'

And here is your third room-mate. His IQ is 100!'

'That's wonderful! We can discuss the latest plays at the theatre!'

Just then another man moves out to capture Albert's hand and shake it. 'I'm your last room-mate and I'm sorry, but my IQ is only 80.'

Albert smiles back at him and says, 'So, where do you think interest rates are headed?'

I've learned:

Written by Andy Rooney, a man who had the gift of saying so much with so few words. Rooney used to be on 60 Minutes TV show.

- That the best classroom in the world is at the feet of an elderly person.
- That when you're in love, it shows.
- That just one person saying to me, 'You've made my day!' - makes my day.
- That being kind is more important than being right.
- That you should never say no to a gift from a child.
- That I can always pray for someone when I don't have the strength to help him in any other way.

- That no matter how serious your life requires you to be, everyone needs a friend to act goofy with.
- That sometimes all a person needs are a hand to hold and a heart to understand.
- That simple walks with my father around the block on summer nights when I was a child did wonders for me as an adult.
- That life is like a roll of toilet paper. The closer it gets to the end, the faster it goes.
- That we should be glad God doesn't give us everything we ask for.
- That money doesn't buy class.
- That it's those small daily happenings that make life so spectacular.
- That under everyone's hard shell is someone who wants to be appreciated and loved.
- That to ignore the facts does not change the facts.
- That when you plan to get even with someone, you are only letting that person continue to hurt you.
- That love, not time, heals all wounds.
- That the easiest way for me to grow as a person is to surround myself with people smarter than I am.
- That everyone you meet deserves to be greeted with a smile.
- That no one is perfect until you fall in love with them.
- That life is tough, but I'm tougher.
- That opportunities are never lost; someone will take the ones you miss.
- That when you harbor bitterness, happiness will dock elsewhere.
- That I wish I could have told my Mom that I love her one more time before she passed away.
- That one should keep his words both soft and tender, because tomorrow he may have to eat them.
- That when your newly born grandchild holds your little finger in his little fist, you're hooked for life.

- That a smile is a cheap way to improve your looks.
- That everyone wants to live on top of the mountain, but all the happiness and growth occurs while you're climbing it.
- That the less time I have to work with, the more things I get done.

Retirement Bonus:

The Navy found they had too many officers and decided to offer an early retirement bonus. They promised any officer who volunteered for Retirement a bonus of $1,000 for every inch measured in a straight line between any two points in his body. The officer got to choose what those two points would be.

The first officer who accepted asked that he be measured from the top of his head to the tip of his toes. He was measured at six feet and walked out with a bonus of $72,000.

The second officer who accepted was a little smarter and asked to be measured from the tip of his outstretched hands to his toes. He walked Out with $96,000.

The third one was a non-commissioned officer, a grizzly old Chief who, when asked where he would like to be measured replied, 'From the tip of my weenie to my testicles.'

It was suggested by the pension man that he might want to reconsider, explaining about the nice big cheques the previous two Officers had received. But the old Chief insisted and they decided to go along with him providing the measurement was taken by a Medical Officer.

The Medical Officer arrived and instructed the Chief to 'drop 'em,' which he did. The medical officer placed the tape measure on the tip of the Chief's weenie and began to work back. 'Dear Lord!', he suddenly exclaimed, "Where are your testicles?"

The old Chief calmly replied, "In Vietnam.'

CHAPTER 16

BAR JOKES

The fight:

A bloke sat down at the bar and ordered drink after drink.

'Is everything okay, mate?' the bartender asked.

'The missus and I got into a fight and she said she isn't talking to me for a month!'

Trying to put a positive spin on things, the bartender said, 'Well, maybe that's kind of a good thing, you know, a little peace and quiet.'

'Yeah, but today is the last day!'

The quickest way:

A well-spoken English gentleman went into a pub and asked, 'What's the quickest way to get to Brecon from here?'

The landlord answered, 'Are you walking or going by car?'

The Englishman answered, 'By car, of course.'

'Well, that's the quickest way.' Retorted the landlord.

At the pub:

I was standing at the bar of Terminal 3 when this small Chinese guy comes in, stands next to me and starts drinking a beer. I asked him, 'Do you know any of those martial arts things – Kung-Fu, Karate or Ju-Jitsu?'

He replied, 'No, why you ask me that? Is it because I'm Chinese?'

'No,' I said, 'It's because you're drinking my beer, you little bugger.'

Only one wish:

Two Aussies, Davo and Johnno, were adrift in a lifeboat. While rummaging through the boat's provisions, Davo stumbled across an old lamp. He rubbed the lamp vigorously and a genie came forth. This genie, however, stated that he could only deliver one wish, not the standard three.

Without giving much thought to the matter, Davo blurted out, 'Turn the entire ocean into beer. Make that Victoria Bitter!'

The genie clapped his hands with a deafening crash, and immediately the sea turned into the hard-earned thirst quencher.

The genie vanished. Only the gentle lapping of beer on the hull broke the stillness as the two men considered their circumstances. Johnno looked disgustedly at Davo whose wish had been granted. After a long, tension-filled moment Johnno said, 'Nice going Davo! Now we're going to have to pee in the boat.'

Bloody Queenslanders:

A genuine joke from Queensland, Australia. It is well known that humour is regional, but this is the first joke that I can say is truly a Queenslander:

At a national conference of the Australian Hotels Association, the general managers of Cascade Brewery (Tasmania), Tooheys (New South Wales), XXXX (Queensland), CUB (Victoria), Coopers (South Australia) and Swan Brewery (Western Australia) found themselves sitting at the same table for lunch.

When the waitress asked what they wanted to drink, the GM of Tooheys said without hesitation, 'I'll have a Tooheys New.'

The head of Carlton & United smiled and said, 'Make mine a VB.'

To which the boss of Coopers replied, 'I'll have a Coopers, the King of Beers.'

The bloke from Cascade asked for 'a Cascade, the cleanest draught on the planet.'

The bloke from Swan asked for a Swan Lager.

The General Manager of XXXX paused a moment and then placed his order: 'I'll have a Diet Coke.'

The others looked at him as if he had sprouted a new head.

'Well, he said with a shrug, if you guys aren't drinking beer, then neither will I.'

Better digestion:

Our grandmothers still had genuine knowledge of staying naturally healthy. My granny lectured me about her practical knowledge: 'For better digestion, I drink beer, for loss of appetite, I drink white wine, with low blood pressure – red wine, with high blood pressure – cognac, and whenever I have a cold, I drink Vodka.

'And when do you drink water?' her granddaughter asked.

'I've never been that sick,' was the quick reply.

Sleeping with his wife:

A man walked into a crowded bar, waving his un-holstered pistol and yelled, 'I have a .45 Colt Auto with eight rounds in the clip and one in the chamber. I want to know who's been sleeping with my wife!'

A voice from the back of the room called out, 'You don't have enough ammo!'

Jack Daniels fishing story:

I went fishing this morning, but after a short time I ran out of worms. Then I saw a cottonmouth with a frog in its mouth. Frogs are good bass bait.

Knowing the snake couldn't bite me with the frog in his mouth, I grabbed it right behind the head, took the frog and put it in my bait bucket.

Now the dilemma was how to release the snake without getting bit. So, I grabbed my bottle of Jack Daniels and poured a little whiskey in its mouth. Its eyes rolled up and it went limp. I released the snake into the lake without incident – carried on fishing, using the frog as bait.

Not long after, I felt a nudge on my foot – it was that damned snake with two more frogs.

Life is good.

Retirement planning:

If you had purchased $1,000 of Nortel stock one year ago it would now be worth $49.00.

With Enron, you would have had $16.50 left of the original $1,000 investment.

With WorldCom. you would have had less than $5.00 left.

If you had purchased $1,000 of Delta Air Lines stock, you would have $49.00 left.

However, if you had purchased $1,000 worth of wine and drank all the wine, then returned the bottles for the refund, you would have had $214. Based on the above, the best current investment advice is to drink wine heavily and recycle the bottles.

I'm passing this information on as a public service – no need to thank me.

[Which countries still pay to recycle bottles? I know Australia doesn't.]

Stand on one leg:

I'm just saying, if the police wanted me to get out of the car and balance on one leg to test my sobriety, the least he could've done was offer to hold my beer.

Bar rules:

Him – no shirt – no service.

Her – no shirt – free beer.

Bar trivia:

- Lord, give me coffee to change the things I can change and wine to accept the things I can't.
- Not to get technical, but according to chemistry – alcohol is a solution.
- Dear alcohol: we had a deal that you would make me prettier, funnier and a better dancer. I saw the video – we need to talk.
- Of course size matters – nobody wants a small glass of wine.
- People who wonder whether the glass is half empty or half full miss the point. The glass is refillable!
- On the back of a wine truck is this sign: In case of accident, bring cheese and crackers – lots of cheese and crackers.
- I'm not an alcoholic. Alcoholics need a drink – I already have one.
- Do you know that two to three glasses of wine a day can reduce your risk of giving a shit?
- I've got salad for dinner. Actually it's fruit salad. Well, mostly grapes. Okay – all grapes – fermented grapes – wine. I've got wine for dinner.
- People say that drinking milk makes you stronger. Drink five glasses of milk and try to move a wall. Can't? Now drink five glasses of wine and the wall will move all by itself.
- I don't drink alcohol. I drink distilled spirits – so I'm not an alcoholic – I'm spiritual.
- I only drink a little, but when I do, I turn into another person and that person drinks a lot.
- Drinking alcoholic beverages before pregnancy can cause pregnancy.

- Our beer is as cold as your ex's heart.

Three whales:

I was at the bar the other night and overheard three very hefty women talking at the bar. Their accent appeared to be Scottish, so I approached and asked, 'Hello, are you three lassies from Scotland?'

One of them angrily screeched, 'It's Wales, Wales you bloody idiot!'

So I apologized and replied, 'I am so sorry. Are you three whales from Scotland?'

And that's the last thing I remember

I'm not paying…

Three animals were having a drink in a bar, when the owner asked for the money.

'I'm not paying,' said the duck. 'I've only got one bill and I'm not breaking it.'

'I've spent my last buck,' said the deer.

'Then the duck'll have to pay,' said the skunk.

'Getting here cost me my last scent.'

We don't serve your kind:

Two cartons of yogurt walk into a bar. The bartender, who was a tub of cottage cheese, says to them, 'We don't serve your kind in here.'

One of the yogurt cartons says back to him, 'Why not? We're cultured individuals.'

CHAPTER 17

HIGH TECHNOLOGY

A frustrated employee in front of his laptop, 'Dear Google, please do not behave like my boss. Please allow me to complete my sentence before you start guessing and suggesting.'

Desert island:

A man had been shipwrecked on a desert island for two years when he suddenly noticed a bottle had been washed ashore. Inside was a piece of paper. With trembling hands, he removed the paper and read, 'Due to lack of activity, we regretfully inform you that we have cancelled your e-mail account.'

Mobile phone:

After a tiring day, a commuter settled down in his seat and closed his eyes. As the train rolled out of the station, a woman sitting next to him pulled out her mobile phone. She started talking in a loud voice, 'Hi sweetheart. It's Sue. I'm on the Train. Yes, I know I'm on the six thirty and not the four thirty train, but I had a long meeting. No honey, not with that Kevin from the accounting office. It was with the boss. No sweetheart, you're the only one in my life. Yes, I'm sure, cross my heart!'

Fifteen minutes later, she was still talking loudly. When the man sitting next to her had enough, he leaned over and said into the phone, 'Sue, hang up the phone and come back to bed.'

Sue doesn't use her mobile phone in public any longer.

Low battery:

A man saved his girlfriend's phone number in his mobile as 'Low Battery.' Whenever she calls him, in his absence, his wife takes the phone and plugs it into the charger. Give that man a medal!

This N That:

- My body is experiencing technical difficulties right now – growing old is not fun.
- Nothing makes me feel so old as having to scroll down to find my year of birth.

Welcome to the 4th Industrial Revolution - the Exponential Age.

- In 1998, Kodak had 170,000 employees and sold 85% of all photo paper worldwide. Within just a few years, their business model disappeared and they went bankrupt. What happened to Kodak will happen in a lot of industries in the next 10 years - and most people don't see it coming. Did you think in 1998 that 3 years later you would never take pictures on paper film again?

  Yet digital cameras were invented in 1975. The first ones only had 10,000 pixels, but followed Moore's law. So as with all exponential technologies, it was a disappointment for a long time, before it became way superior and got mainstream in only a few short years.

- It will now happen with Artificial Intelligence, health, autonomous and electric cars, education, 3D printing, agriculture and jobs.
- Software will disrupt most traditional industries in the next 5-10 years.
- Uber is just a software tool, they don't own any cars, and are now the biggest taxi company in the world.
- Airbnb is now the biggest hotel company in the world, although they don't own any properties.
- Artificial Intelligence: Computers become exponentially better in understanding the world. This year, a computer

beat the best Go player in the world, 10 years earlier than expected. In the US, young lawyers already don't get jobs. Because of IBM Watson, you can get legal advice (so far for more or less basic stuff) within seconds, with 90% accuracy compared with 70% accuracy when done by humans. So if you study law, stop immediately. There will be 90% less lawyers in the future, only specialists will remain.

- Watson already helps nurses diagnose cancer, four times more accurately than human nurses. Facebook now has a pattern recognition software that can recognize faces better than humans. In 2030, computers will become more intelligent than humans.

- Autonomous cars: In 2018 the first self-driving cars will appear for the public. Around 2020, the complete industry will start to be disrupted. You won't want to own a car anymore. You will call a car with your phone, it will show up at your location and drive you to your destination. You will not need to park it, you only pay for the driven distance and can be productive while driving.

    Our kids will never get a driver's license and will never own a car. It will change the cities, because we will need 90-95% less cars for that. We can transform former parking space into parks. 1.2 million people die each year in car accidents world-wide. We now have one accident every 100,000 km, with autonomous driving, that will drop to one accident in 10 million km. That will save a million lives each year.

- Most car companies might become bankrupt. Traditional car companies try the evolutionary approach and just build a better car, while tech companies (Tesla, Apple, Google) will do the revolutionary approach and build a computer on wheels. I spoke to a lot of engineers from Volkswagen and Audi; they are completely terrified of Tesla.

- Insurance companies will have massive trouble because without accidents, the insurance will become 100 times cheaper. Their car insurance business model will disappear.

- Real estate will change. Because if you can work while you commute, people will move further away to live in a more beautiful neighbourhood.

- Electric cars will become main-stream until 2020. Cities will be less noisy because all cars will run on electric. Electricity will become incredibly cheap and clean: Solar production has been on an exponential curve for 30 years, but you can only now see the impact. Last year, more solar energy was installed worldwide than fossil. The price for solar will drop so much that all coal companies will be out of business by 2025.

- With cheap electricity comes cheap and abundant water. Desalination now only needs 2kWh per cubic meter. We don't have scarce water in most places, we only have scarce drinking water. Imagine what will be possible if anyone can have as much clean water as s/he wants, for nearly no cost.

- Health: The Tricorder X price will be announced this year. There will be companies who will build a medical device (called the 'Tricorder' from Star Trek) that works with your phone, which takes your retina scan, your blood sample and you breathe into it. It then analyses 54 biomarkers that will identify nearly any disease. It will be cheap, so in a few years everyone on this planet will have access to world class medicine, nearly for free without an expensive doctor's bill.

- 3D printing: The price of the cheapest 3D printer came down from $18,000 to $400 within 10 years. In the same time, it became 100 times faster. All major shoe companies started 3D printing shoes. Spare airplane parts are already 3D printed in remote airports. The space station now has a printer that eliminates the need for the large amount of spare parts they used to have in the past.

- At the end of this year, new smartphones will have 3D scanning possibilities. You can then 3D scan your feet and print your perfect shoe at home. In China, they already 3D printed a complete six-storey office building. By 2027, 10% of everything that's being produced will be 3D printed!

- Business opportunities: If you think of a niche you want to go in, ask yourself: 'in the future, do you think we will have that?' and if the answer is yes, how can you make that happen sooner? If it doesn't work with your phone, forget the idea. And any idea designed for success in the 20th century is doomed to failure in the 21st century.

- Work: 70-80% of jobs will disappear in the next 20 years. There will be a lot of new jobs, but it's not clear if there will be enough new jobs in such a small time.

- Agriculture: There will be a $100 agricultural robot in the future. Farmers in third world countries can then become managers of their field instead of working all days on their fields.

  Aeroponics will need much less water. The first petri dish produced veal is now available and will be cheaper than cow produced veal in 2018. Right now, 30% of all agricultural surface is used for cows. Imagine if we don't need that space any more. There are several start-ups who will bring insect protein to the market shortly. It contains more protein than meat. It will be labelled as 'an alternative protein source' (because most people still reject the idea of eating insects).

- There is an app called 'moodies' that can already tell in which mood you're in. Until 2020 there will be apps that can tell by your facial expressions if you are lying. Imagine a political debate where it's being displayed when they're telling the truth and when they're not.

- Bitcoin will become mainstream this year and might even become the default reserve currency.

- Longevity: Right now, the average life span increases by three months per year. Four years ago, the life span used to be 79 years, now it's 80 years. The increase itself is increasing and by 2036, there will be more than a one-year increase per year. So we all might live for a long, long time, probably way more than 100.

- Education: The cheapest smartphones are already at $10 in Africa and Asia. By 2020, 70% of all humans will own a smartphone. That means, everyone has the same access to world-class education. Every child can use Khan academy for everything a child learns at school in First World countries. We have already released our software in Indonesia and will release it in Arabic, Swahili and Chinese this Summer, because I see an enormous potential.

- We will give the English apps for free, so that children in Africa can become fluent in English within half a year.

Tech support:

'Okay Bob, let's press the control and escape keys at the same time. That brings up a task list in the middle of the screen. Now type the letter 'P' to bring up the Program Manager.'

Customer: 'I don't have a 'P'.

Tech support: 'On your keyboard, Bob.'

Customer: 'What do you mean?

Tech support: 'P' on your keyboard, Bob.

Customer: 'I'm not going to do that! What kind of an idiot do you think I am?'

Six Truths in Life

1. You cannot stick your tongue out and look up at the ceiling at the same time, a physical impossibility.
2. All idiots, after reading #1 will try it.
3. And discover #1 is a lie.
4. You are smiling now because you enjoy a laugh.
5. You soon will forward this to another person.
6. There is still a stupid smile on your face.

Breakthrough:

Scientists have grown human vocal chords in a petri dish. The results speak for themselves.

Horses Asses:

The U.S. Standard railroad gauge (distance between the rails) is 4 feet, 8.5 inches. That's an exceedingly odd number. Why was that gauge used? Because that's the way they built them in England, and English expatriates designed the U.S. Railroads.

Why did the English build them like that? Because the first rail lines were built by the same people who built the pre-railroad tramways, and that's the gauge they used.

Why did 'they' use that gauge then? Because the people who built the tramways used the same jig and tools that they had used for building wagons, which used that wheel spacing.

Why did the wagons have that particular odd wheel spacing? Well, if they tried to use any other spacing, the wagon wheels would break on some of the old, long distance roads in England, because that's the spacing of the wheel ruts.

So, who built those old rutted roads? Imperial Rome built the first long distance roads in Europe (including England) for their legions. Those roads have been used ever since.

And the ruts in the roads? Roman war chariots formed the initial ruts, which everyone else had to match for fear of destroying their wagon wheels. Since the chariots were made for Imperial Rome, they were all alike in the matter of wheel spacing. Therefore, the United States standard railroad gauge of 4 feet, 8.5 inches is derived from the original specifications for an Imperial Roman war chariot.

In other words, bureaucracies live forever. So the next time you are handed a specification, procedure, or process, and wonder, 'What horse's ass came up with this,' you may be exactly right?

Imperial Roman army chariots were made just wide enough to accommodate the rear ends of two war horses.

Now, the twist to the story:

When you see a Space Shuttle sitting on its launch pad, you will notice that there are two big booster rockets attached to the sides of the main fuel tank. These are solid rocket boosters, or SRB's. The SRB's are made by Thiokol at their factory in Utah.

The engineers who designed the SRB's would have preferred to make them a bit larger, but the SRB's had to be shipped by train from the factory to the launch site. The railroad line from the factory happens to run through a tunnel in the mountains, and the SRB's had to fit through that tunnel.

The tunnel is slightly wider than the railroad track, and the railroad track, as you now know, is about as wide as two horses' behinds. So, a major Space Shuttle design feature of what is arguably the world's most advanced transportation system was determined over *two thousand years ago* by the width of a horse's ass.

And you thought being a horse's ass wasn't important!

Government Theory:

The tribal wisdom of the Dakota Indians, passed on from generation to generation, says that; 'When you discover that you are riding a dead horse, best strategy is to dismount.'

However, in government, more advanced strategies are often employed, such as:

1. Buying a stronger whip.
2. Changing riders
3. Appointing a committee to study the horse.
4. Arranging to visit other countries to see how other cultures ride dead horses.
5. Lowering the standards so that dead horses can be included.
6. Reclassifying the dead horse as living-impaired.
7. Hiring outside contractors to ride the dead horse.
8. Harnessing several dead horses together to increase speed.
9. Providing additional funding and/or training to increase the dead horse's performance.
10. Doing a productivity study to see if lighter riders would improve the dead horse's performance.
11. Declaring that as the dead horse does not have to be fed, it is less costly, carries lower overhead and therefore contributes substantially more to the bottom line of the economy than do some other horses.
12. Rewriting the expected performance requirements for all horses.

And of course...

13 Promoting the dead horse to a supervisory position.

If you don't understand this theory, you haven't lived long enough.

Car wash:

Bill owns a company that manufactures and installs car wash systems. Bill's company installed a car wash system in

Frederick, Maryland. Now, understand that these are complete systems, including the money changer and money taking machines.

The problem started when the new owner complained to Bill that he was losing significant amounts of money from his coin machines each week. He went as far as to accuse Bill's employees of having a key to the boxes and ripping him off.

Bill just couldn't believe that his people would do that, so he set up a camera to catch the thief in action. Well, he did catch the thief on film! They caught a bird sitting on the change slot of the machine. The bird had to go down into the machine, and back up inside to get to the money! Then they spotted him with three quarters in his beak! Another amazing thing is that it was not just one bird - there were several working together.

Once they identified the thieves, they found over $4,000 in quarters on the roof of the car wash and more under a nearby tree.

And you thought you'd heard of everything!! This gives a new twist to the term 'nest egg.'

And to think the phrase 'bird brain' is associated with being dumb. Not these birds!

CHAPTER 18

RULES FOR LIVING

Five undeniable facts:

A wise person once said:

1. We all love to spend money buying new clothes but we never realize that the best moments in life are enjoyed without clothes.
2. Having a cold drink on a hot day with a few friends is nice, but having a hot friend on a cold night after a few drinks - PRICELESS.
3. Breaking News: Condoms don't guarantee safe sex anymore. A friend of mine was wearing one when he was shot dead by the woman's husband.
4. Arguing over a girl's bust size is like choosing between Molson, Heineken, Carlsberg, and Budweiser. Men may state their preferences, but will grab whatever is available.

And last but not least:

5. I haven't verified this, but it sounds legit. A recent study found that women who carry a little extra weight live longer than the men who mention it.

If you can:

- Always be cheerful, ignoring aches and pains,
- Resist complaining and boring people with your troubles,
- Eat the same food every day and be grateful for it,
- Understand when your loved ones are too busy to give you any time,
- Take criticism and blame without resentment,
- Conquer tension without medical help,
- Relax without alcohol,
- Sleep without the aid of drugs,

Then you're probably the family dog!

Words of Wisdom:

'Attitude is a little thing that makes a big difference.' Winston Churchill

'I have the simplest tastes. I'm always satisfied with the best.' Oscar Wilde.

'A little knowledge that acts, is worth infinitely more than much knowledge that is idle.' Kahlil Gibran

'Start by doing what's necessary; then do that's possible, and suddenly you are doing the impossible.' Francis of Assisi.

'An archaeologist is the best husband a woman can have. The older she gets, the more interested he is in her.' Agatha Christie.

'I've never hated a man enough to give him his diamonds back.' Zsa Zsa Gabor

'It's not fair to ask others what you are not willing to do yourself.' Eleanor Roosevelt.

'Be the person your dog thinks you are.' (sign in Vet's office.)

'Do I not destroy my enemies when I make them my friends?' Abraham Lincoln.

'I, not events, have the power to make me happy or unhappy today. I can choose which it shall be. Yesterday is dead, tomorrow hasn't arrived yet. I have just one day, today and I'm going to be happy in it.' Groucho Marx.

'Too bad the only people who know how to run the country are busy driving cabs and cutting hair.' George Burns.

Red faced comments:

If you ever feel a little bit stupid, just dig this up and read it again; you'll begin to think you're a genius.

On September 17, 1994, Alabama's Heather Whitestone was selected as Miss America 1995.)
Question: 'If you could live forever, would you and why?'
Answer: 'I would not live forever, because we should not live forever, because if we were supposed to live forever, then we would live forever, but we cannot live forever, which is why I would not live forever,' Miss Alabama in the 1994 Miss USA contest.

'Whenever I watch TV and see those poor starving kids all over the world, I can't help but cry. I mean I'd love to be skinny like that, but not with all those flies and death and stuff.' Mariah Carey.

'Smoking kills. If you're killed, you've lost a very important part of your life,' Brooke Shields, during an interview to become spokesperson for federal anti-smoking campaign

'I've never had major knee surgery on any other part of my body.' Winston Bennett, University of Kentucky basketball forward.

'Outside of the killings, Washington has one of the lowest crime rates in the country.' Mayor Marion Barry, Washington, DC.

'That lowdown scoundrel deserves to be kicked to death by a jackass, and I'm just the one to do it.' A congressional candidate in Texas.

'Half this game is ninety percent mental.' Philadelphia Phillies manager, Danny Ozark

'It isn't pollution that's harming the environment. It's the impurities in our air and water that are doing it.' Al Gore, Vice President.

'I love California. I practically grew up in Phoenix.' Dan Quayle.

'We've got to pause and ask ourselves: How much clean air do we need?' Lee Iacocca

'The word "genius" isn't applicable in football. A genius is a guy like Norman Einstein.' Joe Theisman, NFL football quarterback and sports analyst.

We don't necessarily discriminate. We simply exclude certain types of people.' Colonel Gerald Wellman, ROTC Instructor.

'Your food stamps will be stopped effective March, 1992 because we received notice that you passed away. May God bless you. You may reapply if there is a change in your circumstances.' Department of Social Services, Greenville, South Carolina.

'Traditionally, most of Australia's imports come from overseas.' Keppel Enderbery.

'If somebody has a bad heart, they can plug this jack in at night as they go to bed and it will monitor their heart throughout the night. And the next morning, when they wake up dead, there'll be a record.' Mark S. Fowler, FCC Chairman.

Water cure:

A woman went to the doctor and said, 'Doctor, I don't know what to do. Every day my husband seems to lose his temper for no reason. It scares me.'

The doctor advised, 'When your husband is getting angry, just take a glass of water and start swishing it in your mouth. Just swish and swish, but don't swallow it until he either leaves the room or calms down.'

Two weeks later the woman returns looking refreshed and says, 'Doctor, that was a brilliant idea! Every time my husband started losing it, I swished with water, and he calmed right down! How does a glass of water do that?'

He replied, 'The water itself does nothing; it's keeping your mouth shut that does the trick.'

[Groan – what a solution!]

CHAPTER 19

ON THE SERIOUS SIDE

Life Lessons:

- If someone treats you like shit, just remember that there's something wrong with them. Not you. Normal people don't go around destroying other human beings.
- Meanness doesn't just happen overnight – it often takes a lifetime of practice to be truly effective.

Six little stories:

1. Once all villagers decided to pray for rain, on the day of prayer all the people gathered, but only one boy came with an umbrella. *That's FAITH.*
2. When you throw a baby in the air, she laughs because she knows you will catch her. *That's TRUST*
3. Every night we go to bed, without any assurance of being alive the next morning but still we set the alarms to wake up. *That's HOPE.*
4. We plan big things for tomorrow in spite of zero knowledge of the future. *That's CONFIDENCE.*
5. We see the world suffering, but still we get married and have children. *That's LOVE.*
6. On an old man's shirt was written a sentence 'I am not 80 years old. I'm sweet 16 with 64 years' experience.' *That's ATTITUDE.*

Change your thinking:

Two men, both seriously ill, occupied the same hospital room. One man was allowed to sit up in his bed for an hour each afternoon to help drain the fluid from his lungs. His bed was next to the room's only window.

The other man had to spend all his time flat on his back.

The men talked for hours on end. They spoke of their wives and families, their homes, their jobs, their involvement in the military service, where they had been on vacation.

Every afternoon, when the man in the bed by the window could sit up, he would pass the time by describing to his roommate all the things he could see outside the window. The man in the other bed began to live for those one hour periods where his world would be broadened and enlivened by all the activity and colour of the world outside.

The window overlooked a park with a lovely lake. Ducks and swans played on the water while children sailed their model boats. Young lovers walked arm in arm amidst flowers of every colour and a fine view of the city skyline could be seen in the distance.

As the man by the window described all this in exquisite details, the man on the other side of the room would close his eyes and imagine this picturesque scene.

One warm afternoon, the man by the window described a parade passing by. Although the other man could not hear the band, he could see it in his mind's eye as the gentleman by the window portrayed it with descriptive words.

Days, weeks and months passed. One morning, the day nurse arrived to bring water for their baths only to find the lifeless body of the man by the window, who had died peacefully in his sleep.

She was saddened and called the hospital attendants to take the body away.

As soon as it was appropriate, the other man asked if he could be moved next to the window. The nurse was happy to make the switch, and after making sure he was comfortable, she left him alone.

Slowly, painfully, he propped himself up on one elbow to take his first look at the real world outside. He strained to slowly turn to look out the window beside his bed. It faced a blank wall.

The man asked the nurse what could have compelled his deceased roommate who had described such wonderful things outside this window. The nurse responded that the man was blind and could not even see the wall.

She said, 'Perhaps he just wanted to encourage you.'

Epilogue: There is tremendous happiness in making others happy, despite our own situations. Shared grief is half the sorrow, but happiness when shared, is doubled.

If you want to feel rich, just count all the things you have that money can't buy.

'Today is a gift, that is why it is called the Present.'

These ads actually existed:

Could you imagine these ads occurring now?

- 'You've won him – now you must keep him – use LUX toilet soap.
- How to measure your wife before buying an ironing table.
- Little white child speaking with a little black child, 'Why doesn't your mamma wash you with Fairy Soap.'
- I can't believe these next ones! To keep a slender figure no one can deny – reach for a Lucky Strike instead of a sweet.
- Enjoy the smooth smoking of fine tobaccos – smoke Pall Mall (shows a picture of Santa Clause.)
- For your health – asthma cigarettes since 1882 for temporary relief of paroxysm of asthma. Effectively treats asthma, hay fever, foul breath (yeah sure), all diseases of the throat, head colds, cancer sores, bronchial irritation. Not recommended for children under 6 (so please encourage those older than 6 to smoke!)

- Cocaine tooth drops. Instantaneous cure. Price 15 cents. For sale at all druggists – March 1885.
- For a better start in life – start cola earlier. How soon is too soon? Even babies thrive on cola. The ideal brain tonic – Coca Cola. (In those days Cola contained cocaine.)

Global warming:

The Arctic Ocean is warming up, icebergs are growing scarcer and in some places the seals are finding the water too hot, according to a report to the Commerce Department yesterday from Consulate, at Bergen, Norway.

Reports from fishermen, seal hunters and explorers all point to a radical change in climate conditions and hitherto unheard-of temperatures in the Arctic zone.

Exploration expeditions report that scarcely any ice has been met as far north as 81 degrees 29 minutes.

Soundings to a depth of 3,100 meters showed the gulf stream still very warm.

Great masses of ice have been replaced by moraines of earth and stones, the report continued, while at many points well known glaciers have entirely disappeared.

Very few seals and no white fish are found in the eastern Arctic, while vast shoals of herring and smelts which have never before ventured so far north, are being encountered in the old seal fishing grounds.

Within a few years it is predicted that due to the ice melt the sea will rise and make most coastal cities uninhabitable.

I must apologize: I neglected to mention that this report was from November 2, 1922, as reported by the AP and published in The Washington Post - 94 years ago!

The exam:

One day, a professor enlivened the classroom and asked his students to prepare for a surprise test. They all waited anxiously at their desks for the exam to begin.

The professor handed out the exams with the text faced down as usual. Once he handed them all out, he asked the students to turn over their papers.

To everyone's surprise, there were no questions – just a black dot in the centre of the sheet of paper.

The professor, seeing the expressions on everyone's faces told them the following, 'I want you to write about what you see on that page.'

The students, confused, got started on the inexplicable task. At the end of the class, the professor took all the exams and started reading each of them aloud in front of the students. All of them, with no exception, defined the black dot, trying to explain its position in the centre of the sheet.

After all the tests had been read, the classroom silent, the professor started to explain, 'I'm not going to grade you on this; I just wanted to give you something to think about. No one wrote about the white part of the paper. Everyone focused on the black dot – and the same happens in our lives.

However, we insist on only focusing on the dark spot – the health issues that bother us, our lack of money, the complicated relationship with a family member, the disappointment with a friend. The dark spots are very small when compared to everything we have in our lives, but they're the ones that pollute our mind.

Take your eyes away from the black dots in your life. Enjoy each one of your blessings, each moment that life gives you. Be happy and live life filled with love!

Switzerland's solution:

Sometimes it's the little things that are most telling. In Switzerland it has long been customary for students to shake the hands of their teachers at the beginning and end of the school day. It's a sign of solidarity and mutual respect between teacher and pupil, one that is thought to encourage the right classroom atmosphere. Justice Minister Simonetta Sommaruga recently felt compelled to further explain that shaking hands was part of Swiss culture and daily life.

And the reason she felt compelled to speak out about the handshake is that two Muslim brothers, aged 14 and 15, who have lived in Switzerland for several years (and thus are familiar with its mores) in the town of Therwil, near Basel, refused to shake the hands of their teacher, a woman, because, they claimed, this would violate Muslim teachings that contact with the opposite sex is allowed only with family members. At first the school authorities decided to avoid trouble, and initially granted the boys an exemption from having to shake the hand of any female teacher. But an uproar followed, as Mayor Reto Wolf explained to the BBC: 'The community was unhappy with the decision taken by the school. In our culture and in our way of communication a handshake is normal and sends out respect for the other person, and this has to be brought [home] to the children in school.'

Therwil's Educational Department reversed the school's decision, explaining in a statement on May 25 that the school's exemption was lifted because 'the public interest with respect to equality between men and women and the integration of foreigners significantly outweighs the freedom of religion.' It added that a teacher has the right to demand a handshake. Furthermore, if the students refused to shake hands again 'The sanctions called for by law will be applied,' which included a possible fine of up to $5,000.

This uproar in Switzerland, where many people were enraged at the original exemption granted to the Muslim boys, did not end after that exemption was itself overturned by the local Educational Department. The Swiss understood quite clearly that this was more than a little quarrel over handshakes; it was a fight over whether the Swiss would be masters in their own house, or whether they would be forced to yield, by the granting of special treatment, to the Islamic view of the proper relations between the sexes. It is one battle – small, but to the Swiss significant – between o'erweening Muslim immigrants and the indigenous Swiss.

Naturally, once the exemption was withdrawn, all hell broke loose among Muslims in Switzerland. The Islamic Central Council of Switzerland, instead of yielding quietly to the Swiss decision to uphold the handshaking custom, criticized the ruling in hysterical terms, claiming that the enforcement of the handshaking is 'totalitarian' (!) because its intent is to *'forbid religious people from meeting their obligations to God.'*

That, of course, was never the 'intent' of the long-standing handshaking custom, which was a nearly-universal custom in Switzerland, and in schools had to do only with encouraging the right classroom atmosphere of mutual respect between instructor and pupil, of which the handshake was one aspect.

The Swiss formulation of the problem – weighing competing claims - will be familiar to Americans versed in Constitutional adjudication. In this case 'The public interest with respect to equality' of the sexes and the 'integration of foreigners' (who are expected to adopt Swiss ways - not force the Swiss to exempt them from some of those ways) were weighed against the 'religious obligations to God' of Muslims, and the former interests found to outweigh the latter.

What this case shows, is that even at the smallest and seemingly inconsequential level, Muslims are challenging the laws and customs of the Infidels among whom they have been allowed to settle [i.e., stealth jihad toward sharia dominance]. Each little victory, or defeat, will determine whether Muslims will truly integrate into a Western society or, instead, refashion that society to meet Muslim requirements.

The handshake has been upheld and, what's more, a stiff fine now will be imposed on those who continue to refuse to shake hands with a female teacher. This is a heartening sign of non-surrender by the Swiss.

The Swiss handshaking dispute has received some, but not enough, press attention. Presumably, it's deemed too inconsequential a matter to bother with. But the Swiss know better. And so should we.

There's an old Scottish saying that in one variant reads: '*Many a little makes a mickle.*' That is, the accumulation of many little things leads to one big thing. That's what's happening in Europe today. This was one victory for the side of sanity. There will need to be a great many more.

Letting go:

- All failed relationships hurt, but losing someone who doesn't appreciate and respect you, is actually a gain – not a loss.
- There comes a time when you have to stop crossing oceans for people who wouldn't jump puddles for you.
- God sometimes removes people from your life to protect you. Don't run after them.
- One of the happiest moments ever is when you find the courage to let go of what you can't change.
  If they miss you, they'll call.
  If they want you, they'll say it.
  If they care – they'll show it.
  And if not – they aren't worth your time.

CONCLUSION

I hope you have enjoyed these jokes and thoughts enough to obtain Volumes 1, 2, 3, 4 and 5 that cover humour and serious thoughts in different areas, so there's no repetition.

Laughter is an essential ingredient to everyday living. If you haven't had a laugh today - you're depriving yourself of enjoyment in life. Bring the jokes out when you're having a bad day - that's what I do. You'll find that things just get better.

If you wish to read books on more serious topics, please see the following information about how to order my other books and e-Books.

www.dealingwithdifficultpeople.info

www.ingramcontent.com/pod-product-compliance
Lightning Source LLC
LaVergne TN
LVHW051553070426
835507LV00021B/2562